Lorenzo by the Ghost Light

A Spiel

Gnashing Teeth Publishing
242 East Main Street
Norman AR 71960

Printed in the United States of America

ISBN 979-8-9854833-6-9

Fiction: Poetry

Gnashing Teeth Publishing First Edition

Table of Ideas Inside

For Larry

Lorenzo by the Ghost Light
Book 1
Scene I
Ghost & Roach & Sphere

I

Some years after the opera shuttered house, home, song,
And holes opened in its roof, a flustered spirit was compelled to say:
"Certainly there must be an echo of aria somewhere near.
But then there is not a soul to hear my shriek, my ectoplasmic bray,"
Sighed this hovering essence.
"Certainly some refrain from Wolfgang Amadeus will suit,"
Said the lone spirit.
"Perhaps one last queen's F, high enough to wriggle our chained rigging?
One dragon's roar, a Tamino sigh, a Papageno/Papagena tweet to boot?"

II

The bearded glimmer hovered about the rigging,
And with translucent limbs kicked at dangling chains:
"There's not a single *Magic Flute* note to be found!
I know old arias clang where curtain creases meet stains,"
Shouted a flustered Lorenzo.
"Very well, I believe I shall argue amongst cat walk dust again,"
Said the ghost.
"I shall snark with specks over drivel like a full-blown ass!
I shall quibble over minute matters triumphantly with selected kin."

III

But fresh from night's purgatory, Lorenzo hovered drowsy,
And he struggled to find the sharpest point with which argue:

"Sunrise after sunrise I am woke in similar translucence.
No matter the issue, I remain right; that is my insatiable view,"
Declared the ghost.
"For example, a wok never runs even when brimming full,"
Barked Lorenzo.
"My kin in the dust say a bathtub with feet can be left running,
But I rightly say you're wet behind the ears! My retort receives a lull."

IV

High in the opera house loft, Lorenzo wins each debate,
And to pigeons above he shouted for the liberation of calamari:
"If I need to, I can do my best Bob Marley rattling chains for freedom.
But I've been known to be unwilling to act, even described ghostly chary,"
Admitted Lorenzo.
"That makes you a Jacob Marley; set your porosity maximus low, let it be rested,"
Said a passing roach.
"B Marley is a precious soul and J, well, that Marley a besieged claqueur.
This I know! I do! I do! This from all the delicious literature I've digested."

V

The Roach pulled up on a long-discarded house curtain,
And boasted he devoured Dickens's complete oeuvre:
"I found it all for the taking, laying shaped as a U heap.
I swallowed page after page, chewed elegantly! I verve!"
Bragged the Roach.
"It was a far tastier text than I have ever tasted before,"
Continued a bug called Hector.
"Libraries are a roach's buffet, fulfilling one's daily fiber need.
It's the pages with the pictures that I most adore."

VI

Lorenzo lowered yet lowered all the more to the roach's level,
And believed he felt a back twinge, somehow a human's sore:
"Hector, you do know this is an opera house without the opera.
That's not Dickens you're eating there but an old Verdi score,"
Shouted the ghost.
"It's one buffet bar after buffet bar, a tasty snack of note,"
Replied Hector.
"The best since I chomped through the Greeks, a dining odyssey.
Though I caught a bit of Achilles in the labyrinth of my throat."

VII

Lorenzo laughed at his friend's expense
And then spilled out the contents of his mind's labyrinth:
"I was filled up full by a love that led to my demise.
Yep! Indeed! Love in Cleveland ended me… oh a fake hyacinth,"
Said Lorenzo running his foot over an abandoned prop.
"Can you imagine what Nicholas Nickleby might taste like?"
Conjected the insatiable insect.
"Certainly it has all the flavors of a Dickens sundae:
The sweet, the theater, more sweet—then later Nick's little tyke."

VIII

Hector fantasized eating page after page, while Lorenzo lamented,
And from the loft a metal object squealed, dropping on Lorenzo's head:
"Ha! You whiney Ghost, you've a grand gel frame halo.
This is what happens when you wander in a theater, obviously dead,"
Said a mouse upon a baton.
"I've been nudging that frame loose for hours just to raise your spirits,"
Said the thrilled Mouse.

"Dorabella! See how it slides down my all, past my porosity maximus.
Make fun with rodent guffaws; I'll haunt you with ghastly visits."

IX

Dorabella, curling her whiskers, nose, mouth into a plotting smile,
And tucking her paws, stood ready to shove stageward a mucked ball:
"What from the heavens can I heave as green as this great fungus
sphere,
Delivering a special splat on a whiney ghost's head after a tremendous
fall?"
Threatened Dorabella.
"The spirit of Stanwyck save me! What green monster are you aiming
my way?"
Shrieked Lorenzo.
"It resembles nothing found at Fenway nor any other special park.
Yet here's a meteorite heading straight past my head, chaotically
stray."

X

In charm the ball had none; in mold it measured in gasps,
And in force it steamed towards Hector at rest on a gleaming glass
harp:
"Good God! Here comes the greenish of moons! Meteorites amok!
Such a rodent-blast from its orbit it flies, sloppy, hardly sharp,"
Shouted the alarmed Roach.
But if I may comment in the short time I have before contact,"
Continued Hector.
"There appears to be a protein quality to Dor's khaki canon fly.
But now I fly for after this breath I will have been smacked."

XI

Dorabella's sphere smashed into the rotting Bruno's Glass Harp
And launched Hector skyward into rattling rigging chains:

"Yahoo! When has a wayward cootie ever reached such heights?
Oh someone measure how high: Mark twain! Mark twain!"
Shouted the Roach.
"Twains measure not in height but depth, dear rotating Roach,"
Said Lorenzo to his friend, now in free fall.
"But it's the glass clinks of which I now obsessively worry
It's clink… screech… clink… screech… clink… screech… that we need
to broach."

XII

Smith's angel harp, perhaps once home for saintly winds whispers
And fragile, like a tune of Hoffman, shattered to the extreme:
"Yes, beef in brightly red sauce once gave this sphere charisma.
But now my ears rattle from Lorenzo's shrilly scream,"
Said Dorabella covering her ears.
"Empirically, this sphere had its origins in the underground,"
Professed the Mouse.
"The evidence encourages by the name on this wrapper.
Though I know of no train station closer than say, Long Island Sound."

XIII

Lorenzo owlishly examined the sphere, bump by bump,
And he came to a conclusion he concluded with dread:
"Fellas and ladies! Legend requests food to invite ghosts to the stage,
But it should be with savory breads, fresh coffee to drudge up the
dead,"
Prospected Lorenzo.
"Muffins with jam, with more coffee, yes… anything less would be
rude,"
Said the Ghost.
"I sense no luscious scents wafting about, no invitations to the sweet.
Just petrified spoils of stagehand food on which to brood."

Drooling, Hector scuttled the length of the last pin rail
And descended a counterweight rope to rest upon its lock:
"Save the ball! Save the ball! Green balls are succulent aged
Especially, for roach's palate, stagehand verde, served with a stout bock,"
Called out the roach.
"The finest gatherers from the finest nests would say in candid measures,"
Added Hector, whistling.
"Serve found green balls with bits of broom, along with dust bunny relish.
Add just a pinch of crushed dust mites and voila! a grand dining pleasure."

It was Lorenzo, however, who insisted on attention at this moment,
And he blew Hector's praised delicacy into a dark corner:
"Theater gods insist whistlers remain silent or doors knocked upon accordingly.
But this! This shattered harp turns me into the Linden Opera House Mourner,"
Raged Lorenzo.
"Foul thunder answers the Bard's Scottish King when called out indiscreetly,"
Warned the weathered one.
"Dorabella, with your paws, you have plucked the Devil's triple pause,
Releasing three haughty spirits—Diabolus in musica—into a horrific spree."

Book 1
Scene 2
Dorabella & Find & Dining

I

The House of Dorabella was never divided, but opened by a hole
And through this which she grew from pink pup to opera house diva:
"From this ledge I shall Tosca leap from this grubby top.
From the cushion below I will land or all shall sit soprano shiva,"
She directed when Tosca was on.
"From this hole I can only now see cold rain slapping the stage,"
Murmured the Mouse.
"The hole in our roof is bringing in all that is not needed, I see,
And still it is I, and only I, that sent that devil tune thing into a rage."

II

Dorabella reflected upon her special birthplace—under a silverware
tray.
And throughout her puphood, she was shown places to poop:
"I was born with several silver spoons above my head, not to mention
knives.
Oh! the chiming heard at each sunset, spoons, forks taken away by
group,"
Reminisced Dorabella.
"As pups we huddled, three brothers, three sisters, pink, squirmy little
pups,"
Daydreamed the Mouse.
"Then my dear brother, Bruce, left the nest to become a famed
biologist.
We imagined Bruce at work mixing, brewing about all sorts of oddly
shaped cups."

With one paw, she dragged a little Smith's angel glass,
And, with consternation, considered the biology career of brother Bruce:
"Words upon air say Bruce now floats luminescent for his years of biology labor.
He stars in his own jar, supervising solutions trekking sluice to sluice,"
Said the Mouse in tragic smirk.
"Oh Brother Bruce, such sacrifice, such derring-do. Then you said to look to Brother Steve,"
Said Dorabella, sifting through angel harp shards.
Oh Brother Steve! So kind and considerate, he trained as a great veterinarian.
He had one dedicated patient, a calico named J. Wilks! That's all I know, I believe."

Pawing splinters, Dorabella feared stirring demons from centuries long sleep,
And quivered though she only found a prism jetting between jagged:
"My sister, Roberta, sang higher than any angel harp.
Yet ill behavior all about her left her spirits ragged, crushed, bruised,"
Thought Dorabella.
"Ah but there is Brother Fred, alley explorer extraordinaire!"
Mused the Mouse.
"No matter waves of snow, sleet, nor wads of melted spearmint stuck to paws,
Fred remained dedicated to quest, to hear his beloved soprano—he a claque debonair."

V

Dorabella sobbed for Brother Steve, Brother Bruce, Sister Roberta,
And marveled at Fred's frank advice as he departed:
"Never go poo in a silverware tray; it gives you away.
Beware steely tunnels; you'll slide into an abyss, broken-hearted,"
Said Dorabella of her advising brother, Fred.
"But, of course, my ears acted smaller than most mouse ears,"
Recalled Dorabella with a smirk.
"Huddling with shining silver! Oh, so intoxicating to me since I was pup.
My grandest step up from cupboard rodent to inquisitive mouse
pioneer."

VI

The theater at midnight resumed its empty ring,
And silence split only by the occasional clap of rain:
"It's always in winter when I make my most horrific mistakes,
Thus my exile from the house of Kibitz for raising a little cain,"
Confessed Dorabella.
"Warmth! I sought out warmth with a snuggle by the silver,"
She continued.
"Rattle! A lovely rattle! I figured Ravel's 'Bolero' upon spoons with
paws.
Such a hot tune, it lead this Mouse to quake then quiver."

VII

Dorabella deeply reflected on her departure from the house of Kibitz,
And, spying bits of ice spewing from the loft, admitted regret:
"Such a warm and cozy place we had with Mr. and Mrs. Kibitz,
Friendly words followed by effusive words followed by... but yet..."
Wallowed a reflective Mouse.
"They talked quite fondly even about their nagging Aunt Shamata,"
Smiled the Mouse.

"Excited, I sought to join in on topics like Scioto snow.
With wiggling butt edging wooden butte, I caught a whiff of ricotta."

VIII

Dorabella's whiskers curled with the divine scent of cheese,
And she quivered over fanciful scents of carved mozzarella:
"Manna from Heaven shaped heavenly, mice-beloved lasagna!
Yes, here come the drools! Stars! Stars! Oh, it's all gastro-stella!"
Reflected Dorabella, her nose rising high with the memory.
"But there would no lasagna! No noodles! No cheese… not a molecule of sauce,"
Mourned the Mouse.
"Spotting my tail, Mr. Kibitz fired to the ceiling a coloratura squeal.
He smashed a butter knife, ending my concertized 'Bolero', a multicultural loss."

IX

As days with mice found in silverware drawers go, so did this one,
And in flight, Dorabella twisted towards a kitchen window valance:
"From midair I saw all the Kibitz family delights—a table set for many.
Judging from their enchanting linoleum floor this was not a house of malice,"
She described.
"As I swung from the valance, the Kibitz team spoke in fastidious terms."
She said.
"I heard shouts of pest, vermin, creepy-crawly, not to mention, I think, matzah ball.
Worst of all, I heard 'Mice carry pestilence, swarms of unwelcomed germs!'"

X

Shocked at her reception, Dorabella let go of the purple valance,
And fell to the floor, just missing swipes of pie rolling pins:
"Ducking under a crevice, I heard shrieks: 'Call the cats! Call the cats!'
Now their cats I liked. We often napped together… their coats such a
cozy inn,"
Said Dorabella in full paw embrace.
"Oh, such was once a warm, magnificent home, the House of Kibitz,"
Said Dorabella.
"One with chats, grub, candle light… but its air now heavy from
swishing pie bats.
The landscape before me was daunting, ending with a vent held
jaggedly by loose rivets."

XI

For Dorabella, the riveting science of vents suddenly registered,
And as she panicked, she promised to one day take up vent
scholarship:
"From the look of the scene, loose rivets sink mouse seizure schemes.
I may be fresh from the nest, but a screw loose presages a fateful trip,"
Determined the Mouse.
"I plotted a dash from crevice to vent, while the Kibitz couple yakked
of tea,"
Said Dorabella.
"Cup of tea? Rosehip or rooibos? Tulsi or gingko? How's about
ashwagandha?
The Kibitz tea list was so long that I knew a great variety would set me
free."

XII

Out from the Kibitz crevice, Dorabella dashed for the faraway vent,
And she heard, one last time, the Kibitz clan chatter each to each:
"Sage or valerian root? Dandelion or marshmallow root? Pine needle or peach?
Then Mr. Kibitz said Peach! Mrs. Kibitz, you're a Peach! You're a Kibitz Peach,"
Chimed the Kibitz couple.
"Peachy! Ugh! Squeezy peachy! Bile rising! Huggy peach! Oh screech,"
Said, play by play, by Dorabella.
"They both said, 'Peach! Peach! Peach!' So I dashed… dashed… dashed!
They're kissing! I'm dashing! They're squishing! I'm bolting! They're… vent…reach!"

XIII

Dorabella squeezed through the vent's grill, leaving a tuft of bloodied fur,
And began spiraling downward, pinging against furnace aluminum walls into the abyss:
"I heard beloved Kibitz voices fading with 'Want to see our new dust ruffle?'
'A dust ruffle!' I'm blushing! 'A… ruffle, Maury!' Ah… cheeks pink… a kiss,"
Reported the embarrassed rodent escapee.
"'Did you know,' I said to the hard walls: 'aluminum—Atomic Number 13?'"
Said the descending Mouse.
"Since I received no answer from the walls, I continued to fall.
Until landing heavily beside an old cauliflower floret painted sage green."

Thirteen does not always mean ill luck; Dorabella found a needed feast,
And starved since a breakfast of sourdough crumbs, she devoured the floret:
"Cauliflower florets are Elysian fleurs… bubbling, luscious, musculus fleurs.
I say to ye old botanical blossom, to my belly ye shall go; I orate,"
Said Dorabella, chewing cabbage flower muck Bolognaise.
"Oh, how blooms glide about the Palate, a diner's petite amuse,"
Drooled Dorabella.
"Oh, how pretty mots spooled from a Mouse who never parle Francais,
When I spied, spying on me, a ghastly face in the furnace tunnel haze."

XV

The Mouse trembled at the sight of spirit with a sliced mustache,
And resolved a trip to the silverware drawer ushered in her day of demise:
"I seem to fear you more than any spirits, but that's another tale.
You're quite the translucent imp, most likely evil, yet looking wise,"
Muttered Dorabella
"Now that you have found me what do we do? What do we do?"
Quivered the Mouse.
"Will I run as you plot to chase? Will I stay matching Mouse to Ghost eyes?
Will you devour me whole then chase me down with a phantasm's brew?"

Book 1
Scene 3
Roach Voices, Specter Voices

I

Cold rain fell on the Linden Opera House stage, pinging scattered glass,
And Dorabella finished revisiting how she met Lorenzo:
"The phantom studied me by brushing mustachio remains.
'I am more of a sprite without spite, hardly a loathing ghoul, you know,'"
So recalled Dorabella.
"He said to me! Right to me! 'It's time for you be in an opera house, Mouse,'"
Said Dorabella.
"'Understand I am one more interested in matinees than malevolence.
Enter guardedly; we'll search for arias. Welcome, Mouse, our house!'"

II

A whiskered Galahad, Dorabella's quest for arias stretched through winter,
And only abandoned sandwiches, dust, rope appeared... nary an aria or duet:
"I searched a tunnel, from stage to abyss, checking brick to cracked brick,
The sharp clay alarming me as those at the Kibitz Bris—pacing, with slicing fret,"
Noted the opera house knight.
"Ah the elephant ramp! Arias were never sung here! But tears... a plenitude of tears,"
Said Lorenzo.
"Oh the tears remain! They roll in streams down the sides of the elephant wall.

Streams cascade still from misused pachyderms? Sad toughs slogging through years?"

Dorabella cornered Lorenzo plucking baroque notes from tormenter curtains,
And she chewed his ear over the misery, each detail of a storm in brew:
"The more the rain pummels the loft, the more the elephant walls cry.
Now that I have failed to find arias, what do we do? What do we do?"
Wailed the Mouse.
"We make coffee. We don't have coffee? Very well. We'll imagine coffees,"
Replied Lorenzo, distressed.
"We'll fancy Turkish! Savor Ethiopian! Relish pure golden Columbian!
Oh my! Then follow it with chocolate chasers! Yes! Add delightfully melted toffees."

Up from angel harp wreckage, Hector buzzed into the conversation,
And fluttered his roach wings in deep consternation:
"I ascertain from years of roach-ness, this veteran roach knows,
Whisper Columbian, I say on behalf of the Periplaneta Americana Nation,"
Exclaimed Hector.
"Many circles carry odd inklings about the doings of dioecious cannibalistic,"
Said Hector, exuding protective tones.
"Your meaning is lost, old Ghost, even speaking of mice missing caffeine.
As Head Roach of this joint: Add nonsensical notions as your crank statistic."

Hector cringed at Lorenzo's lividness, his moods of grouchiness,
And, as the ghost snarled, "Columbian!" his spirits hovered the angel harp:
"SHshSHshSHshSHshSHshSH! See smashed glass!
They'll rise, Roach, rise from a world beneath any scavenging carp,"
Said Lorenzo in shaky, spearing speech.
"We all must take care with our words these days; they reveal! They reveal,"
Cautioned the Ghost.
"Within these decayed walls, crafty ears perch to catch careless comments.
It is with insipid intentions your freedom they seek to steal."

VI

The Roach settled on the wounded angel harp's handsome frame,
And spoke of roach's life from the shine of an oak dais:
"My prospects expect a shoe or two mashing me daily.
Whether wing-tips or quiet puppies, it's a mashing from stylists,"
Bemoaned the detested cucaracha.
"A loafing roach need beware the approaching rubber sole,"
Warned Hector.
"Foot shadows, news rolled into mallets, all of which I abhor.
Weapons of roach destruction simply since we slime, nay crawl."

VII

Hector stood at edge of the harp, falling water pinging a solemn tune,
And he voiced with the sincerity of Brando's Antony:
"Ghosts! Mice! Dust bunnies! Tune your antennae.
I whine not over mashed bugs, but in boast of roach destiny,"
Elocuted Hector.
"A crushed roach smears… dreadfully oozes on men's shoes,"

Emoted the Roach.
"Juicy souls smear fancy soles, for bugs have no bones.
Such is the cockroach fate; such is the stage for cockroach blues."

VIII

Hector hummed a woeful warble, believing he was a harmonica,
And he shook his winged body, relishing morbidity without haste:
"If you step on us, do we not squish? If you spray us, do we not wilt?
Set murderous traps, dare I quiver? Plant poison, dare I taste?"
Orated the Roach, with six Bernhardt-like legs.
"How might a Roach sway this Ghost, manipulate this Mouse? Sway dust?"
Queried the bug.
"Stand for muck! Holler in mire! Celebrate the insect phantastic!
Hail the six legged! Revel on rust... share the crust?"

IX

Spying fossilized rye, Hector surrendered the angel harp dais,
And squatted alongside Dorabella's preciously pebbled crumbs:
"Bravo, specter! Da capo shade! You've killed an F, sharply.
Remedies for poor Smith's angel... well there's a scratch on a roach's bum,"
Taunted the Roach.
"Oh! Hector, shall you be chased about these walls for a boodled cuisine of sounds?"
Asked Lorenzo.
"Let it be known that all my Fs remain sharp; they proudly puff green.
Yet sure as I muse over glass... I hear voices at our door... with hums and pounds."

X

At quick glance, Lorenzo studied shards from the damaged angel harp,
And brushed a finger across his frosted hemi-stache:
"Had I only passed on with both sides of that thick, blond mustachio.
I'd have a stupendous Cupid's bow, furry to each end in match,"
Lamented Lorenzo.
"Instead, I passed with having one side fall off in the bitter cold,"
Recalled the Spirit.
"One day I shall reunite the two ends as one feisty set of whiskers.
For now I've shards to move and an injured harp to remold."

XI

The humming and pounding grew ever so louder
And Ghost, Mouse, with Roach, squeezed into a corner to hide:
"Glory be! I believe it's my operatically fried brother home to roost,
But what does he bring into the house but bunny and gloomy monster wide,"
Remarked Dorabella.
"Now they hop, bop, prance as shadowy behemoths before my ghost light,"
Said an alarmed Lorenzo.
"Forsaken theaters do babble, even rumble, but this escapade appears absurd.
One can but hope they'll soon be pounding and humming out of sight."

XII

The secreted trio scrutinized the intruders dance about the beloved lantern,
And, in fury, Hector juddered, Dorabella shook, Lorenzo drooled ectoplasm:

18

"Such a haughty trio presuming to haunt my light; they thieve our shadows.
Look how they strut! Look how they twist, all tomfoolery, nay grotesque spasm!"
Proclaimed the Ghost.
"I am certain that my brother, Fred, brings the tallest shadow,"
Said Dorabella, softly.
"Quick! Veil the Roach! Secret the Mouse! Shroud the Ghost!
The voices take their shadows: a Monster, a Mouse a Hare are on the go."

XIII

The festive voices faded as they forced their way through a crusted door,
And their essence continued within Dorabella like a cinematic flicker spread:
"I fear Fred is drifting further and further in search of his soprano.
She will never sing for him solely; she will never know he was Fred,"
Said Dorabella, tearfully.
"I, myself, shall be off to dream once more of dear Veronica Lake,"
Purred the Roach.
"I would happily drown in her peekaboo! Sun beside her fiery heart.
Then by moonlight… we loving chewers… we'd devour cake upon cake."

XIV

Silence filled the old opera house, save a water drip center stage,
And the Linden Avenue troika emerged from their dark corner:
"Lake again, Roach? There is much more to say of B. Stanwyck's beauty!
Note her majestic, her carriage courageous, you hexapod street scorner,"
Argued Lorenzo, easily lured into this dispute.

"Empty barneys blow widest when from the brashest of intonations,"
Interjected the Mouse.
"You argue over goddesses whose shadows can only be found as flickers.
Should spoilt seas swamp cities, you'd still revel in futile consternations."

XV

Face to face, the Ghost & Bug could hardly keep their color,
And, despite the rise of three demons from the broken harp, they bellowed:
"Lake! No B! Lake! No Stan! Lake! No Wyk! Ah the flesh, oh the fantasy!
B! No Lake! Stan! No Lake... isn't this romantic? From this we've never mellowed,"
Said Roach then Ghost, full of shouts & pouts.
"Feces in pieces, such blather squeezes, wheezes, whines insipid breezes... dread,"
Said one of the Demons atop the harp.
"Prepare! (Sneezes!) Prepare! (Sneezes!) Sniff... prepare (Sneezes!)
Excuse! Prepare for opera house gloom from Chort, Murmur, & Ed."

OLIO #1
Chort's Lament

La Di Da Do! Welcome to my night seize.

Despite my horned handsomeness, I am a Chort short of Mephistopheles! Ha! La Di Da Do! Please, before the we begin the show, unwrap anything that crinkles, let go any necessary wheeze.

On behalf of my master dance master, Beelzebub, and in light of all October expectations, I arrive through the Harp to spread November fears. I am a reminder, sordidly and sagely, that
Octobers hang brutal for demons such as me, a Chort. Here is my dance.

La Di Da Do! I went to the doctor and the doctor says, "You'll live to be 60!" So, I says, "Doctor, I am 60!" And the doctor says: "See! What did I tell you?" La Di Da Do!

I sing La Di Da Do... La Di Da Do... La... oof damned hoof arthritis.

La Di Da Do! We've unplugged the old opera ghost's light.

How many Chorts does it take to screw in a lightbulb? Chort! Chortle! Watt?

A humor bone is stifled when you're deep in the dark.

La Di Da Do! Once in hell a damned fellow said, "Devil doctor! Devil doctor! It hurts when he does this to me." The devil doctor said..."keep doing it!" La Di Da Do...

La Di Da Do! I'd rather be the light.

Book 2
Scene I
Hoofing Legends

I

Encased in a cold's congestive grip, Demon Ed spoke in rasps,
And he fired projectile snot as his envied super power would:
"Mine, ahem… mine, ahem… HACK… Mine seeps as a perpetual condition.
I see you… see you… HACK… as an opera house penumbra misunderstood,"
Coughed Ed.
"My first night seeing the Dark of Night, since '32; Oh! Stage, I've missed you,"
Continued Ed.
"I'm blubbing. Oh blubbing Ed! Blub! Blub! Flood the Earth! Flood the Earth! Blub!
Even a pathetic demon, now and then, might be in desperate need of a tissue."

II

Before the company the melancholic demon dropped pear size waterworks,
And Hector kindly pointed an old paper napkin once only blown by gust:
"Excuse me while I empty a demon's clogged respiring canals.
Funny word, 'blow', the gathering of a clearing wind or a mistake, I trust,"
Said Ed, wiping at evasive nostril crust.
"My day passed in '32, when the Commendatore called upon Don Giovanni,"
Recalled the stuffy imp.

"Ill-timed sleep prevented my demon's entrance… (Sneeze!) my stage days at end.
Not a singer or super felt my absence; nay, none from the robust to the scrawny."

III

The Ghost, Mouse, even the Roach looked about awkwardly,
And each began to whistle tunes, though only Hector managed pitch:
"Shush! No hush! No ease, man, ease! Allow for pesky advice.
Seek the Café Sans Chairs, where lay glass mounds, reflective, rich,"
Snorted Chort.
"Beer bottles, passing especially gleam, make delightful angel harp spares,"
Continued the hoofed and horned monster.
"As sure as I adore my papa Bog, cheap brews offer the classy glass.
Out from my swine-like façade pluck long hairs; in popping pain I'll swear."

IV

Chort danced with Murmur, their hooves clacking a horrific tap,
And Ed tossed his brother demon a pan for grotesque clanking:
"Mine! Only mine! Mind you, mine… are this opera house's only sounds!
Expert ears flip-flap over mine jazzy hooves; for this you'll twist in thanking,"
Chortled Chort.
These boards make for rough rugs on which to cut; it's hoof splints I dread,"
Said Chort.
"Babble consumes brains in the passageways of this quagmirical night.
Allow me to share the tale of our demonic firm, Chort, Murmur, and Ed."

Chort's searing tale opened with steam firing from his flopping ears,
And he encouraged Murmur to reveal the dreaded Wall of Wasted Whimsey:
"Murmur made me build and build until stones and earth made for a grand arch.
Says Murmur to me, 'Move stones to exit your Hell, your soul restored directly,'"
Narrated Chort.
"Hazes in blazes! Palls in sprawls! Murmur rides from the depths on a feathered fellow,"
Reported the demon in snorts.
"Though his ride steps sleek, with the gait of a ferocious feline,
Murmur speaks softly, so very softly, he'll never bellow."

VI

Duke-like in sash, Murmur stepped forth, saddle-sore from a rough griffon ride.
And he addressed Lorenzo adroitly, succinctly, words wet with drool:
"You sir, without pupils, appear desperately in need of a final home... a home... a home....
Endlessly wandering crushed opera houses, a torture, insipid, awfully cruel...cruel...cruel..."
Muttered Murmur.
"My own purpose is to aid your soul to its rest; why waste another hour... hour... hour?"
Choked out Murmur.
"Legions of creatures follow my rumbles; trumpets might announce me.
I drool, Chort snorts, and Ed...well Ed sneezes; we've each our power... power... power..."

Dorabella's fur stood straight. She shrieked with a shocked throat,
And she edged ever so further away from Murmur's raspy rhythms:
"Each of your whispers rattle about my ears as ever so hideous.
I need wash them clear with more pleasing sounds or a Hanby hymn,"
Remarked Dorabella.
"My verse on Earth blasted free through Franklin's howling Harp... Harp...
Harp..."
Replied the decked-out Demon.
"I am now; shall we kill the fatted calf or it leave it to rot... rot... rot?
I confess I name drop; a skill for one soared over a scarp...scarp...
scarp..."

Hector's antennae waved at unprecedented speeds,
And even the opera house Roach took careful backwards steps:
"Roach! I've a special appetite for wretched, pitiable, melancholy.
It's my guidance into oblivion that restores spirits to pep,"
Came the Murmur.
"Steal for me stones of the Union Station arcade; bring them to the Wall of
Wasting Whimsey,"
Commanded the whispering creeper.
"Chort, once a star of the much ignored Hot Pepper Hoarding Demon
Circuit.
Submit me your souls, Ghost, Roach, and Mouse; he'll dance a vaudevillian
frenzy."

Chort bashfully looked at his chipped hooves, a fiend in mighty blush,
And Ed joyfully rolled gobs of phlegm between his jagged teeth:
"Shucks, Murmur, such were my flops on Orpheum's Hades Circuit.

Such midnight rambles! But shoosh! Never tell Albee and Keith!"
Said a humble Chort.
"Ha! Ha! Demons in the temple were we! From Keith's to Crystal Hall,"
Boasted Chort.
"Such midnight follies along the Valley of the River Faux Vivre.
Days sleeping in Baltimore & Ohio coal cars… Hot damn! What a ball."

X

Chort twirled his curly hair, sloppily smacked his hooves onto the
stage,
And he recalled crushing the Peanut Circuit boards with authoritative
smut:
"Malice grew as the proper dance; all gentle ones were tossed out.
Call our gambols insatiable… nay foul… nay revolting, leaving opera
house rut,"
Recalled the faux hoofer.
"We had no art; but we had teeth, eating when we were bored,"
Said a smiling Chort.
"Oh! Voix de Ville… we devoured the gentle leaving split bone & lore.
With bloated bellies we villains chortled as an accomplished hoard."

XI

Lorenzo, convinced Chort's fable arrived with bleak meaning, let go a
sigh,
And he addressed the three fugitive devils two eyes to forty eyes:
"Opera house monsters, blanketed thick in self-indulgent phlegm…
Our ears burn from your nonsense, your yelps, your horrid cries,"
Called out Lorenzo.
"West of this Ville sits a tea house, draped by a pawpaw's green
shawl,"
Bargained the Ghost.
"Reset my ghost light, direct me towards this gray stone abode,
There to conjure a spirit's memoir by gnawing an old buckeyes haul."

XII

Dorabella considered Lorenzo's desire to nosh on nuts with eyes,
And she shook herself clean, having been hosed by Ed's snotty spray:
"Demon Ed, mind the river pouring impolitely from your mouth.
Demon Murmur, mind your scratched throat, such wheeze and hay!"
Recommended the mannered Mouse.
"Demon Chort, show us to the Wall of Wasted Whimsey, bliss's
insistent stead,"
Continued the Mouse.
"We'll forge for seamless flutes, a cure for our anguished harp.
"Then we can move a stone or two, if I might find my brother Fred!"

XIII

The demonic triptych howled in three part harmony, appalled by
Dorabella's audacity,
And Ed misfired from his triple-caved snout, dousing Chort with a
wallop of snot:
"Oh haggle Mouse! Broker your whiskers! Broker them until they bend
and break.
We expect Whimsey Wall stones brought hither; your Fred we care
naught,"
Barked Chort.
"Bring the stones from the arch to the opera house; leave not a speck
of dust,"
Commanded the fury imp.
"Return the Whimsey's granite to where tenors once swooned over
sopranos.
Brick up its walls for silence, where demons shall rule with delicious
distrust."

XIV

Lorenzo's boney finger combed his frosted whiskers,
And considered the burden of moving stone, splinter, shard:

"I've neither the arterial or the vein but I've a vigorous phantom heart.
Moving stones to bring misery to this house... for that I must be on guard,"
Conveyed the Ghost to his opera mates.
"Negotiate demons Chort, Murmur, Ed, allow your odious souls blossom,"
Continued Lorenzo.
"Oh that we should own Sisyphus' back; we are but rodent, bug, ghost.
 I am a gleaming pixie more measured by teaspoons more than Old Possum."

XV

With one whisker dipping into his mouth, Lorenzo gathered his strength,
And addressed Chort, Murmur, keeping a steady eye on sloppy Ed:
"By all that's sacred... Stanwyck, theater, tea... we'll oblige the Demons.
We'll set for West of the Ville where I shall retrieve my humble Ghost cred,"
Proclaimed Lorenzo.
"Let's step from the opera house for the night, free Mouse, free Ghost, free Roach,"
Said Lorenzo.
"The alley door's the right hole, crushed out by ice, wind, or earthy creature.
Shield your heads from the storm; icy rain falls... a subject we need broach."

Book 2
Scene 2
Oodles of Noodles

I

A rusted hot dog stand lay in the rain, blocking the alley at Front Street,
And yet its signage still read 'Noodles Hot Dogs! OODLES OF NOODLES':
"From my home I ooze into the rain! From my home I seep into the wet unknown!
Dorabella, bounce stone to stone. Use brick and bottle, kit and caboodle,"
Said a determined Lorenzo.
"Find ample trash on which to stand, worried Roach. Watch the rising water,"
Warned the Ghost.
"Watch for the sleeping alley man, the rain rising about his heavily whiskered face.
We need raise him from his concrete bed, this precious yet strange squatter."

II

Hector studied the hallway of the man's nose, comparing antennae to nostril hairs.
And Dorabella climbed aboard, with a plan in her throat:
"Fred said, to revive abandoned men, one need blow Puccini through noses.
I know the Café Mouse Moo tunes from La Blow Ahem! Mot by Italian mot,"
Announced the grainy-voiced gnawer.
"This one hair rivals my antennae impressively, quite in fact, imposingly,"

Said Hector in swift analysis.
"How does air flow through such passes to rival tall grasses in Kansas?
Mouse sing to sew through these wavy hairs… stress them succinctly."

III

Dorabella blew into the man's right nostril what Puccini she knew,
And wind flowing from the left nostril blew Hector into the misty night:
"Oh mine ears have never caught old Giacomo as such an off-pitch recitation.
Your mousy warble… dare I say dulcet sound… oh so in tune with fright,"
Commented Lorenzo,
"Thank you kindly, kindly Ghost, you give a choral mouse an ego boost,"
Responded Dorabella.
"This hideous ice night covers the city's hideous news.
I sadly report this harried man shall be forever here left to roost."

IV

Lorenzo floated past the comatose man; Dorabella followed with rapidly petite steps,
And Hector worked his way back, fighting wind, rain, and a ravenous crow:
"Eat worms you bag of pitchy caws, maws, and spindly claws!
Dunk your feathered-brained head in the river; ride the Scioto ice flow,"
Shouted the Roach to his predator.
"Look, you jester-eyed Job! There goes the ghost of old Edgar Allan Poe,"
Said an alarmed Hector.
"There's no meat within my weathered shell; I'm merely roach and brains,"
Pleaded Hector.

"Now I see, crow, it's crushed squirrel you admire, bones and rodent meat.
If it's the dead you wish to devour, then yes, carry on! Feel no social strain."

V

Lorenzo considered Hector's desperate situation, flicking his mustache,
And spied a three masted ship inelegantly floating south, crushing dock after dock:
"It's an odd night for a sail, but to each must find what floats their own boat.
Mine eyes have faded from yearly dust, but is that boat led by a fowl flock?"
Observed the mystified Vision.
"This truck's sign reads with spice: 'Noodles Hotdogs! Eat Oodles of Noodles!'"
Read Lorenzo.
"The thought! Munching on a dog! It makes my shade fragrance ready to spring.
"Atop! Van Gogh strokes of yellow… no brown… Oh blessed seed! Hey a poodle!"

VI

There laid a crushed poodle, its fur moldy yarn, red splashed about grey.
And from its middle rose a growling hound ghost, snarling a shaggy dog yarn:
"Lo… woof… I was a copious doggie… bark… a renowned, revered growler.
Lunch break from dogged service called… for my palate a hint from the farm,"
Spoke the spirited creature.

"Just for a hint of beef! A taste! An ample sample! A beef baby on a bun,"
Said the Hound.
"Reckless diligence filled my pores! A hound dog rocket, I pursued this aromatic cart.
Through icy gales, I dashed… all fours above ground… yet I was doomed to be done."

VII

The recently passed Poodle failed at reaching a nagging itch,
And mournfully recalled the results of his compulsive decision:
"As sure as I prided myself as Pietro the Guiles Street Poodle,
Whoa, bemoan the tides of canine and standing cart collision,"
Howled Pietro.
"BBBOO! GRR! I now stand an eerie Dog. BBBOO! GRR! BBBOO! GRR!"
Snarled the Dog, for he had little teeth.
"I said to you all mere mortals: "BBBOO! GRR! "BBBOO! GRR! ITCH
I say again! "BBBOO! GRR! Oh itch! "BBBOO! GRR! Itch! AHH! PRRR!"

VIII

Lorenzo, Hector, even Dorabella, paused for a moment, amazed,
And then all three laughed, hooted, even guffawed at the rather green ghost:
"I trained with the finest poltergeists, licensed apparitions, phantasms Ph.D degreed,
All under the auspices of specialists—a very particular academic host,"
Boasted Lorenzo of his spectral credentials.
"You, Poodle Ghost, have just emerged in spirit with little bite or menacing snarl,"
Advised the former opera house resident.
"Learn when to howl like a derecho wind, when to skulk in appropriately gloomy shadows,

When to ooze ectoplasm, when to scratch upon walls, nails a ragged
gnarl."

IX

Dorabella continued laughing, this time at poor Lorenzo's conceit,
And she laughed so hard tumbling backwards into the hot dog truck
hole:
"There's nary a dog in here; Nor sits a cat hair, nor even a bun crumb.
Here sits a hollow wiener stall--quite unable to pacify any hungry soul,"
Said a disappointed Mouse in an echo.
"How to fathom Pietro's fate; no hearty beef junk—a swerve followed
by clunk,"
Chewed Dorabella.
"Wait! Wait! Here's a bun! Wait! Yet another! Buns cracked right down
the middle!
Bun! Buns! Buns by the river. Delightful river-buns! Oh such danged
luck."

X

Pushing the poached bun through the hole, Dorabella met chemistry,
And she watched in horror as icy rain dissolved the doughy tube:
"How can I froth over my labial palp? How can I drool past me max
palp?
Great starch stream! Suck up the starch! Suck up the starch! Ya boob!"
Barked Hector.
"Oh a stench about my spiracles! How can you let such treasure melt
on?"
Shrieked the Roach.
"Stop the rain! Stop the rain! For all that's holy in my precious cercus'
hairs.
It's melting! It's melting! Oh what a storm... destroy my wicked
brawn..."

Mustering his best Sarah Bernhardt, Hector gasped, spun, sputtered histrionically,
And as his six legs pointed straight into the iced night—an imagined bug's death:
"I am La Tosca! Oh Art! Oh science! Oh my empty, forsaken gut!
I jump at aria's end! Oh hunger! We ache before God! I utter all one breath,"
Sighed the seasoned theater bug.
"Your quest, brother Roach? Don't let fade the evil firm of Chort, Murmur, & Ed,"
Chimed in Lorenzo.
"Oh Hector, your belly is not an empty vessel; those starving twist about elsewhere.
These are the times to pursue the right glass; then there will be days for bread."

XII

Hector settled by the ghost Poodle, Pietro, whose muzzle out-whiskered Lorenzo,
And Dorabella pulled herself from the gash in the frankfurter cart, she in a huff:
"The darkness within this beef can booms like the harsh core of Chort.
Finding one Mouse arguing for any sign of the irradiated would be rough,"
Explained Dorabella.
"Soaked behind ears Mouse! That stale dark has the right angle and bark,"
Interjected Pietro.
"Find its right side, then roll forward to a ghost hound's fantasy home: fantastic Fiji.
We've a wonder van! It crescendos about hills, floats when rivers rise brutal, stark.''

36

XIII

The Roach's magnetism proved hardly enough to set the cart on its
wheels,
And Dorabella's sneezed with each push on the cart's metal carcass:
"Tell us, spirited Poodle! We need the right glass to corral the worst of
Demons.
Our angel harp crushed by a petrified meatball. Do opera gods curse
us?"
Queried Lorenzo.
"A hellish pastiche of demons demand stones from the Wall of Wasted
Whimsey,"
Continued the degreed spirit.
"Our labors fall to gathering stones, repair the harp, squat about a
beloved tea house.
Yet with the wall sealing the old opera house, leaving it barren and
chintzy."

XIV

Pietro drooled green ectoplasm, shook his coat, howled at the icy
clouds,
And he lifted a ghostly hind leg high hoping to launch a steady stream:
"To bark or not to bark; woof! there's the needed rub against this
deathly state.
Ah the futility of non-existence; perchance to feel through paws—a
dog's dainty dream,"
Said the anguished hound.
"Hercules had twelve burdens, whilst you arrive modestly with only
three,"
Continued the dead dog.
"I know a fading arch, sans dolphins, but with stone and scattered
glass.

There you can fetch hardy stones, good patching glass, even aim a satisfying pee."

XV

Pietro pawed the hot dog cart, noting it was all downhill to the fabled arch,
And futilely inhaling, Lorenzo exhaled dust, readily giving the cart a poltergeist push:
"Heave Pietro! Heave Hector! Here I go Lorenzo! Here's a Mouse's contribution.
I'll pinch myself in reverse, thrusting from my miniscule but mighty mouse tush,"
Said a revved up Dorabella.
"Granted rodent G-force seems slight, but I remind all: mice rarely appear fickle,"
Grunted the Mouse.
"Within this van we can glide for Pietro's arch, obtain needed glass, requested stone.
Here comes my butt thrust. Hop on; be ready to ride right out of this pickle."

Book 2
Scene 3
Father Giblet's Savory Service

I

Dorabella's rump delivered the right thump with exact force, a
veracious nudge,
And the cart up-lifted from concrete to wabble upon four squeaky
wheels:
"It's an upstarts quartet, racing for glory in a hot dog cart for a singular
arch.
Hop aboard, Mouse, Hound! Hector, man the navigation; Let's all swap
ghost spiels,"
Shouted Lorenzo.
"First, I'll rattle of the mailman delivering bills through mounds of
green July snow,"
Spoke Lorenzo first.
"A morning squall rattled sidewalks, direct, quite the eerie.
Upon his shoulder, a leather bag stuffed with royal-typed lines, perfect
row by row."

II

The quartet stampeded aboard the Oodles of Noodles pushcart,
And with a nudge from the Mouse, the cart rumbled up high:
"Throw all weight left; roll right; check your nerves' height.
Bark loudly at crowds though there be none nigh,"
Called out the Pooch.
"Bare feet swollen, scabbed, dressed in a holey coat of blue colors,"
Spoke up the theater Ghost.
"Old Bill delivered papered burdens leaving each household in a good
funk!
A foreclosure here! An overdue invite there! The stuff of day mired in
squalor."

III

The Ghost Poodle guided the Oodles van around a corner at Spring Street,
And nicked the Baltimore & Ohio overpass pillars, punting pebbles plus a lost quarter:
"To your right, mice and bugs, you'll see the famed spot of a pen long gone.
Old Sparky's home, not to mention Ohio's gift to letters. Oh? His name? Senior Porter,"
Announced the self-appointed tour guide Poodle.
"But there is my frozen Mailman Bill to consider, to ponder, upon which to dwell,"
Interrupted Lorenzo again.
"Through snowy, fluttering July holiday streamers, Bill wandered into a brickyard ruin.
Short of breath, Bill took a rest at edge of a pit, relishing a church bell's knell."

IV

Once darkened clouds parted, revealing a moon slice, sprinkled by a faint stars bent,
And the cart zipped by a neon dispatch: "Midnight Dream Special - $12.00 reuben and fries."
"Catching air, Bill spied a man bearing dust, dressed in a bright coat of yellows, reds, more.
'Are you Joseph, an angel of dreams? Or are you my dream weaver, teasing and wry?'"
Said Lorenzo, quoting Bill.
"'I'm neither angel nor medium,' he said to Bill. 'I am Joseph, the man, a Mulby's brickmaker,'
Replied the messy man to Bill," so said Lorenzo.
"Yet, you gleam like a silver quarter in the palm of a hungry child,"
Said Bill quite desperately.

40

"Advise me Elijah, Joseph, angel in one. Advise me how to carry. I have hot despair.
Delivering ill news day to day… What wisdom do you have within your head so wild."

V

The Oodles cart arrived at the Union Station Arch as per Pietro's directions,
And Lorenzo brought Bill's tale to a succinct, say, a proper denouement:
"Joseph, who foresaw the world's hunger, cleared dust from his lips.
'Well…' said Joseph"… according to Bill… "'Pop pimples privately, son,'"
Said in accordance by Lorenzo.
"'Wash your knees, uh, wisely. Eat not the dust coating of your labors as any dining course,'
Said Joseph to postal fellow Bill.
'But, uh, most importantly, uh, keep your bottom clear of strangers' sharp corners.
Then, when snoring to bother your wife, trust wild dreams to clear away your remorse.'"

VI

Graupel torpedoed about the arch in union with a bitter wind,
And pelted Hector, Dorabella, while Pietro nipped at dodgy flakes:
"Joseph sneezed, wiped his nose upon his yellowish sleeve, then took leave.
Bill knocked earth from his knees, taking stock of all significant stakes,"
Said Lorenzo, tearing up.
"Indeed, Bill, bewildered by a prophet's visit, discerned he heard well enough,"
Noted Lorenzo.

"'This is a vision in need of honor,' said Bill. He said this indeed.
Indeed, in honor of such a visit, he even named his son Lorenzo
Joseph."

VII

Lorenzo's audience let loose a vigorous applause for the tale,
And yet Hector found fault in the telling after stomping six feet in clap
and howl:
"How many times will you utter indeed, Lorenzo, try an indubitably!
No an indisputably! No an incontestably! Roll your air with the greatest
vowels,"
Instructed the Roach.
"Crunch your consonants constantly; rumble pomposity from your
belly,"
Advised the self-appointed forensics expert, Hector.
"Epics like these come with the price of cloying review, be aware! Be
aware!
Live performance is never for the feint hearted nor those with skins of
jelly."

VIII

Dorabella surveyed the arch, ignoring the Roach's uninvited theories,
And through the harsh wind she heard a shrill whisper, frightened,
tragic.
"Pardon me, Mouse. Can you help a fellow foul down on his luck?
The rafters are all on the lam, vanished from the farm as if magic,"
Piercing the air in a pitiable plea.
"Dorabella Mouse, to whom do you… Heavens! That's a big chicken!"
Shouted Hector in surrender to what the night offered.
"Ah! I suppose I am a roach who bugged out and seen a fantastical
world.
Such glorious roasters, pans at the ready; strike up the oven, open the
kitchen."

42

Hector dreamed of a feast, with all the trimmings served about arch squatter,
And from the shadows came hefty Fowl, who introduced himself as Schmaltz:
"This here fellow we call Gribenes, but at a distance; he smells of onions.
Never mind his words, for he appears always a tad fried; the least of his faults,"
Whispered Schmaltz to Dorabella.
"Mama called me Gribenes, though I preferred the moniker, Benne Scraps,"
Explained a humble Turkey.
"Got into scraps. Lots! Rumbled with a young turk called Schmaltz-- see."
"That would be me," interjected his co-bird. "That would be him. Wanna scrap?"

X

Both birds took to rumbling, sending feathers about the fog-drenched arch.
And amidst horrific gobbles, there came a powerful voice, splitting the bout:
"Schmaltz! Schmaltz! Schmaltz! Grotesque Gribenes! Both pecked from the rafters.
Recall that over stuffing yourself is a sin. Be leery of uninvited dressings. Keep stout,"
Said the voice of the preacher bird, Father Giblet.
"Brother Roach! Sister Mouse! Fellow Ghosts! We're a rafter on the lam from holiday tables,"
Continued the extraordinary Turkey.
"Our hearts can be fried or tossed—that you can gobble... but there's a slicker path to choose.

Set claws on drive, children. Run! Run for a better fate than my poor
beloved Mama Mable."

XI

Father Giblet stood upon a blue bottle for a pulpit, shaking his reddish
snood,
And his brown feathers blended with the arch's columns invisible:
"Once devoured, it is a short journey through darkness. Your very
shape altered,
Brothers and sisters... I sense a foul apocalyptic lurky, ready to cleave
us divisible,"
Sermonized the revered Bird.
"By my grandfather's wattle, by the pluck of his wizened beard,"
Continued the cleric, concisely.
"Be not a lamb! Lie not next to yams! Deter mushed gourds tartlet!
Waver not! These requests should not appear as so weird."

XII

Street light yellow bathed the arch, spotting Father Giblet's pulpit,
And holiday bulbs framed the latest minster in beauteous yellow and
blue:
"Shake your eighteen! I speak for the anatomy of the Turkey, wings,
coverts all!
We're a rafter not a herd! November third Thursdays are days to rue,"
Hollered Giblet.
"Curse the noon hour we becomes sandwiches with mustard and
cheese,"
Stomped the bird.
"Curse Fridays after, to be at pieces in a leftover orgy! (Two Turkeys say,
'Gobble! Gobble!')
We're not mixed with mushroom soup, poured steaming over rice!
Please!"

XIII

Father Giblet, bounding off his pulpit, drew Lorenzo's attention the blue glass bottle,
And as Giblet preached, chants echoed off the neighboring coffee shops, boutiques.
"Dear birds: November ushers in the end of times. (*The rafters utter 'Gobble! Gobble! Gobble!'*)
Yet by your humble beaks, know there is an answer, all should not seem bleak,"
Lectured the rafter priest.
"Run to your cousins in Narragansett, the old Norfolk flock! Run Bronzes and Browns!"
Advised Father Giblet.
"We've feet! We've wings. Give thanks for your sprint... Run Royal Palms! Take flight!
Or it's the growling gullet for all! Going down! Going down! Chewed up! Going down!"

XIV

Screaming wretched 'gobbles,' hundreds of frightened bird scattered about the arch,
And Dorabella followed Hector into the blue bottle in avoidance of being stomped:
"Coverts, wattles, Tom's got eighteen feathers to shake. Trot my children! Trot!
We're mighty birds not fried Bucyrus bologna at the ready to be chomped,"
Called the Father to his fleeing congregates.
"Ghosts lose their taste for the bird! Stay still! It's holidays that haunt!"
Pleaded Lorenzo into the foul mayhem.
"Stay, wander with ghosts, mice, even roaches! We've now the right glass!
Now we can all go together to grand tea: stay it's just a short jaunt."

45

Lorenzo knew he bore witness to ten thousand turkeys trotting madly,
And nudging the blue bottle into the Oodles cart, he gave testimony:
"We're a lonely quartet again, I fear, on our way to the West of the Ville.
Still, there's much to accomplish, sure as I stand near Nationwide and Marconi!"
Pronounced the opera Ghost, storing the bottle with a precise poltergeist tap.
"We'll ride up the old 3-C, tossing obliges at my old Linden home,"
Continued Lorenzo, calming three listeners, for the Turkeys were long gone.
"Through my very own ectoplasmic gas will ride up to a plum tea house.
We'll pay homage to a fabulous water fall; it's all resourcefully uphill we roam."

OLIO #2
Murmur's Lament

It's my garble... gutter muddle... utter Murmur mangle ....

... my voice. It's not my font. It's how I talk, like a wet violin. Oh, violins. Do you get my words? If you get my words, please return them at your earliest convenience.

What is the worldly way to explain my time in this space, this stage, this house unlit? Evilness makes me drool. It's never a happy drool, such is the way of cats. I would devour lava to have a cat. I have a pig... a demonic pig. I have three of these pigs... and they sing old love songs in a three part harmony. Oh, to sip molten rock; to have a cat.

It's apparent I'm a little weak on the horrifying part of my job. Inside the world we crawled from, I am teased without mercy. Then again, where we demons crawl, mercy is a quality never blessed. I'm glad to be out of that world but I am sad that I fail at monstering every time.

It's garble... or Grable... or Gable... it's futile snark when I am hardly able.

But so much mayhem I might orchestrate. I'm out for exquisite mayhem, the mayhem of bows and strings under Chort and Ed's trumpeting vibrato. Oh, to shake the rafters.

Garble! Garble! Garble!

BOOK 3
Scene 1
Moon Chats

I

Under the dim light of a wispy moon, the quartet heard fading gobblers,
And Father Giblet's sermon withered as he chased one bird then another:
"Repent, for that's the word I seem to know. Gobble! Gobble! Gobble! Repent!
Yet how might a turkey repent? Why do I even utter repent, repent? Um… er…"
Came the diminishing Father Giblet opine.
"Find Cincinnati! Flee for Cincinnati! Seek to settle as a bird of different feather,"
Faded the preacher bird's call.
"Wait! Wait for me! Forget Cincinnati! They cook turkey dogs.
Gloom! Fowl! Doom! You withered wanders in harshest of harsh weather."

II

Father Giblet's once booming voice drifted away, leaving a silent street,
And the last of the rafters faded with one final call; "He gobbles the truth!":
"Brings a Roach to singing—Puccini! I've not the Dvorak chords.
Still, a tune because of the moon… perhaps a toast with a twisted vermouth,"
Cheered the happy Roach.
"Abundant Ghosts, pretty, pretty Mice… there's none of you that shall find sleep,"
Sang Hector, bleating out an off-pitch "Nessun Dorma."

"Let's cruise the Oodles machine to the old Pub Dube, the one lit in blue up high.
A calamari nosh awaits… mounting plates, Fried! Curled! Deep!"

III

All were crouched inside the Oodles van except a stretched out Roach,
And under a fading moon, they rolled away from the arch:
"The river is down while the tea house is far, far up an Ohio hill.
Find an avenue bearing west, with a slight Cleveland edge for the march,"
Directed a cramped Lorenzo.
"Let go of the old Pub Dube, Hector; roaches risk drowning in shot glasses,"
Warned the Ghost.
"I see your beads of ectoplasmic sweat, Pietro, we need an emergency stop.
For you, here's a proper pole, one surrounded by the tallest of grasses."

IV

Pietro wagged a sliver of a tail, stretched into an enviable down dog,
And aiming at a "No Parking" sign, he lifted a translucent leg for enchanting pee:
"Grow, garden of weeds, grow! From the spirits of dogs, accept my streaming gift.
By the sweet lady-by-the-lake, rise brambles, buttercups, here at least an urban lea,"
Howled a soothed Pietro.
"Worts galore, mother and mug, I dribble tactfully beneath a slender moon,"
Boasted a relieved Ghost Hound.
"Join me, Hector! Climb aboard, Mouse! Together we'll praise all things lunar.

50

Call us a Dvořák Trio, a bass, a bass, with mousy coloratura, in doting croon."

V

Dorabella made her way to the spirited Dog, hoping for a lift up by way of tail,
And once above the Ghost Dog, she sank nose, tail, and whiskers into weeds:
"How can I not but pass through… way through the valley of a dog gone ghost?
I fear no canine, see pooches as pooches, ignore mongrel growling breeds,"
Considered the Mouse.
"Instead, I'll be Mouse Gallahad! No, Whiskered Lancelot… No, Beady-eyed Gawain?"
Muttered Dorabella, falling deep in thought.
"Sir Ector de Maris? Sir Brunor le Noir? Sir Lebius Desconneu?
Oh the Grail I seek: a lovesick opera Mouse… My head throbs, such strain."

VI

Dorabella curled in the tall grass, dreaming of a knight-like quest.
And groomed her nose, imagining herself as Arthur's Knight, Ector de Maris:
"Perhaps Fred shipwrecked… oh horrible storm… as did Tristan at an Irish shore.
He will I rescue, with joy, from any vicious guard, from Rome to Paris,"
Fantasized Dorabella.
"A Maris Mouse quests sixty-one days exact, adorned in chainmail bangle,"
Surmised the Mouse deep into the night.
"Perhaps Brother's caught within crevices of ramshackle opera palaces.

A search it shall be... one in need of candles from an ancient chapel mantle."

VII

The newly knighted Mouse took a long glance at the falling moon slice,
And sans bangle, sans sword, sans shield, she met her enemy--The Green Exterminator:
"Ah ha! In your green chapel I have wandered, brought here by rodent destiny.
A swish here, followed by an inverted jab somewhere, you jaded mouse hater,"
Sparred Dorabella, rustling away in grass.
"I see you aiming hose & spout, your tank of death nestled upon your back,"
Snarled the Knight Mouse to her menacing vision.
"Tease me, taunt me, should I secrete my miniscule hide in chapel corners.
Curse me! Scare the hell out of me. Can you cut a Mouse a bit of slack?"

VIII

Battle-ready, Dorabella plucked a blade of grass to duel said exterminator,
And she howled at the moon when she realized she carried a green sword:
"My allegiance to King Author! For without whom I'd be Mouse sans home.
A dandy king, a round king, a plucky bespeckled, lunatic king who hoards,"
Said the valiant knight in miniature.
"So it is Mouse you seek to slay; from your weed of jeans, red flannels to dread,"
Bespoke Dorabella to the tallest blades of grass.

52

"But do you fear, decrepit Green Exterminator, the trial of a holiday joust?
I bear Christmas tinsel hauberk attire, ready to defend the honor of my brother, Fred."

IX

Dorabella received neither battle cry nor fright from the waving crabgrass knight,
And she sparred with spiky green blades, stalks glistening from yellow streetlight:
"Your name, horrid exterminator, Your name? Tis your head I fail to chop.
Winter's on the rise! Like Gawain, I tackle you in frost, a moonlit Mouse Knight,"
Pondered Dorabella, knowing that lyrical mice with salt never just ponder.
"My toes clasp earth, a tin lid my shield, it's the Green Exterminator I shall blot,"
Smirked the Mouse.
"It's shield spectacular, with a spent Kent's-shaped pentangle,
Like Gawain's adorned shield, I bear a badge—Solomon's Endless Knot."

X

Dorabella twisted, turned; her spasmodic thrusts were spotted by her friends,
And Lorenzo leaned in closely to watch the Mouse's fantastic fight play:
"Halloween is never past. I've turned trash to dress, buffer, blade.
I shall ride fair Pietro as my gringalet. Just like the questing knight by day,"
Spouted the Mouse, joyously unaware she was being watched.
"Perhaps a hunt to snag a stag or tear at a boar might be in order,"

Boasted Dorabella, smacking her tin lid shield.
"Together, Hector, upon Pietro we'll ride as the disgruntled Vermin
Gang.
I, a guiding light for chivalric rodents, we'll glide to the West of Ville
border."

XI

Pietro joined the mustached ghost to witness Dorabella the Good,
And Lorenzo determined mice will duel when shuffling through grass
thickets:
"Beware, Dog and Theater Spook! Beware the Exterminator's Danish
Axe.
Be brave, Sir Hector Roach. This gang shall defend spider, ant, and
cricket,"
Declared Dorabella, a blade of grass extended on high.
"Thou gristle giant! Thou boil of a foil! I bite my paw at thee, you devil
spawn…"
Said the Mouse growing more and more exhausted.
"Thrust! Thrust! Thou venomous toad! Oh such literary wars call for a
nap.
Scurvy foil toad… yawn… you six foot foe… meet a three inch…
yawn…"

XII

Eyelids drooping, Dorabella slid down into the grass for sweet school,
And Lorenzo, that brilliant poltergeist, lifted her into the Oodles van:
"Our grand knight has gone night-night. Her snores echo fraught
battles.
She faced the dread Exterminator, like Gawain at the chapel, honored
her clan,"
Said Lorenzo, covering the mouse with a gyro wrapper.
"Mice now sleep, roaches scuttle, the night draws to its bleakest
shade,"
54

Mused Lorenzo, turning his head skyward.
"There, through the city light drain you need strain for Andromeda.
There we can seek West of Ville, protected by Dorabella's sharpest grass blade."

XIII

The avenue whispered stories, through square houses, brown lawns, rusted gates,
And a sturdy breeze whisked Lorenzo about the street, blurring the stars:
"Whoa! South… Yes south, see a winged horse on his head… Enif, his sparkling nose.
We've dozens of Cleveland blocks to traverse… the road shall bump & jar…"
Said Lorenzo to Pietro as well as the Roach huddling nearby.
"We need trip away contrary from Pegasus' glimmering celestial schnoz,"
Resolved the ghost to his companions.
"Zoom from the south, away from interstellar foals and fish.
Tea house remedies to seal away demons remains our knightly cause."

XIV

Lorenzo fired up the Oodles van, dodged a crater here, ten more there,
And Pietro whispered to Dorabella's ear, dropping ectoplasmic drool in her ear:
"Never ride upon a ghost dog's back, Mouse. You'll sink to the mud.
This is grand advice, sleepy face, yet you can only say 'Num! Num! Num! Here!'"
Said the Dog, setting about a warm corner.
"Pisces floats as a kneeling tenor, a tortured tenor, starved, poor knish,"
Thought Lorenzo, eyes linked to the stars.

"He's like Charles' enslaved Samson at the mill, exhausted from the grind.
Distraught tenor, hair cut as did Delilah to poor hippy Sam; Hearts!
Let's follow the fish!"

XV

The Oodles van swerved just as a chain of rats darted across the avenue,
And, as each held another's tail, the lead shouted, "We're frightened here!":
"Why, I must ask, why need I cover the keys of the angel harp?
Why? Chort, Murmur, & Ed haunt our house with hideous swear & sneer,"
Said Lorenzo, softly, through his drooping broken mustachio.
"All three curse, stomp, litter our palace with malice deep,"
Lamented Lorenzo as Pietro stuck his head out the van door.
"Precise glass is prescribed, found; now in vanity a memory tea I pursue…
Dodge rats, chase demons… these are street things while the sensible sleep."

BOOK 3
Scene II
Avenue Knights

I

With hushed politeness, the Vermin-Ghost Gang churned north to the Ville,
And Pietro, thrilled with the moving van, savored the wind flapping his ears:
"Oh so many sleeping neighbors need be seen on this blasted avenue.
We of mongrel-kind appreciate breeze grandeur; we are beholden window sears,"
Barked the Ghost Dog in crisp bass-baritone.
"Dorabella chose the right knight; like Gawain on holiday, I gather equal mirth,"
Said the dog, his tongue madly bending sideways.
"Watch, Roach! Watch, Ghost! How I drool on Avenue in the straightest of lines.
Woof! Engine House Number 18! Woof! Wake up snoozing Earth."

II

Pietro grew alert as the van zipped past oodles of crossroads,
And he spied the four corners certainly hiding guitar players sealing deals:
"Oh… the signs! All screaming of horrific this act and sinful that act.
Planned outrage! That's what we see! Planned outrage! That's how I feel,"
Snarled Hector, noting leaning billboards.
"Oh, if Mr. Johnson came to play on these corners, I'd curl up by his feet,"
Mused the deceased Mutt.

"I'd savor every earthly tune Mr. Robert might muster, even howl if
cued.
A dog loves a lick, a guitar kiss blue, a dog's ear worm played sweet."

III

In a flash, Lorenzo's ensemble eclipsed the crossroads of Mulby, then
Myrtle,
And, in fabulous tease, establishments offering dishes of Firfir, Kitfo &
Tibs:
"I'd have a pleading roar in my belly had I not died years' end in '89.
I crave a simple taste… yet no gastric plumbing exists between my
ribs,"
Lamented Lorenzo, rubbing where no belly bounced.
"Through a short life, I rattled as a bag of bones, flesh stretched upon
skeletal posts,"
Said Lorenzo with a wry smile
"Oh, I could eat, devour, drink coffee until I shook high under the
midnight sky.
Here I am this night, a Ghost on a hot dog van… now who are these
other ghosts?"

IV

In the bricked divides between hair braiding salons, by a church in a
shack,
And rising over the Trey's Leaning Tower of Used Tires tin roof, spirits
rose:
"See here, Brother Lorenzo, the opera house is down, return to your
Linden place.
Consider deeply, Lorenzo, how, though death grabbed you, your
station grows,"
Said an oddly shaped Spirit.
"The virus has left—died away—left with only shame… its whole
brood,"

58

Noted the Spirit, now oddly shaped another way.
"It ravaged you, blighted your eyes to white; yet for many you are a sweet vision.
So haunt honorably, Lorenzo… uh… haunt with a better mustache… sorry to be rude."

V

Eyes lovingly silver, Lorenzo surrendered thoughts of his missing empty stomach,
And smiled with ghostly pride when he noticed the oddly shaped spirit forlorn:
"Your sadness grips me, fellow Spirit; what troubles you on the avenue of your haunt?
Had I tear ducts, I would cry a flood, massive like the March day I was born,"
Asked Lorenzo studying the misshapen presence.
"Oh… dear Lorenzo, I drift nightly, dissatisfied in my haunting practice,"
Replied the Mass, melding into a polyhedron.
"In early years as a shade, I procrastinated over which opera house to haunt.
Unresolved, I chose the wrong house, doomed to pester Mrs. Boyd's jabbing cactus."

VI

Lorenzo moved to bite his lip to suppress a laugh, but his teeth laid into his chin,
And Hector let out a snort, though roach snorts are seldom heard:
"Why so wrapped as a polyhedron? Why so many varied shapes, Spook?
You recall my passing all too well, image by image in a word,"
Said Lorenzo, realizing his Linden Opera House fortune.

"Why it's my best defense. Who'd consider to disbelieve a polyhedron?"
Replied the Mass, his eyes projecting in Picasso-like directions.
"Should I not cause dread, terror, or fright, I may cease to exist.
I am a Math Spirit; I conjure dread in the doubting geometric heathen."

VII

In streetlight, the Vermin, with the Ghosts, spotted Ebenezer's First Church,
And Hector barked along with Pietro, letting all know this is what night dwellers do:
"So the old curmudgeon sought redemption in a turkey, he did. Or was it a goose?
A broch tzu dirt! –a curse! December television & it's a triple spirits' visit you rue,"
Said Pietro, letting go a dickens of a growl.
"Pietro! Pietro! Oh, Pietro, you mix your Ebenezers making you a misguided Mutt,"
Corrected Lorenzo of his traveling companion.
"Ebenezers abound, risking limbs for a safe haven beneath a starred Heaven.
You may be the king of ghost barks, but your judgment's detoured into a rut."

VIII

A wildly whiskered Ghost Muse rose above the Ebenezer First Church,
And with splendid teeth, matching any Cheshire Mouser, he flashed a grin:
"Opera House Mouse Queen, Dorabella, it's your loving Uncle Aidel.
I've gone the way of Ghost Church Mouse, devout repentant of all my rodent sin,"
Said the Uncle to his beloved niece.

"Uncle Aidel! Dear Uncle Aidel! From a spirit's eye have you spied my brother, Fred?'
Squeaked Dorabella in gleeful curiosity.
"I can speak of the luscious pulpit wood I gnawed and of hymnals quite delicious.
There's a menu I highly recommend for its soulful food; hunger I need not dread."

IX

Uncle Aidel placed his paws over his eyes, wiping glowing tears away,
And he delicately pulled at an obstinate splinter pierced between his two front teeth:
"No dear, I've seen much but so little of the opera which contains Fred.
Not since my former form had I seen him, chewing an aged Christmas wreath,"
Reminisced the Uncle.
"Such green teeth had Fred for days to follow; just desserts for a holiday snacky,"
Continued Aidel, still nagged by the splinter.
"Mouse dining, Dorabella, preciously provides our world its poise,
So never nibble on the dead, not finger, not toe! Such is a deed of the tacky."

X

The once living Mouse began to descend like a moon exhausted after midnight,
And blowing kisses to his niece, he dropped towards the old Ebenezer:
"I've got to find what makes us splinter! I've got to find what makes us splinter!
Farewell, Opera Mouse Queen… savor the varied! So says this deceased geezer,"
Advised Aidel as he vanished into the church.

"Such a handsome Uncle, tightly tuned whiskers—a withered yet wise Mouse,"
Said Lorenzo, slipping into a friendly funk.
"Math Ghost, I gather from these haunts we each roll well in the love scheme.
Your shapes show in hazy beauty, despite your drifting into the wrong house."

XI

The Spirit balled up in third form but pulled an ectoplasmic sciatic nerve,
And he rolled about in howling agony, darting across the murky skies:
"Charlie horse of the dead! Charlie horse of the dead!
Oh, this then that, all due to accumulating years; up next, eyeball styes,"
Shouted the Spirit, dropping dignity for street-wise pity.
"Lorenzo, I sense that I've much to gain by the jabs of desert fruit,"
Said the shapely Spirit, taking a howling break.
"So a haunting I will go, for what else can a poor ghost do?
Hugging a cactus prompts my spirit never to be a horrifying brute."

XII

Refiguring as a spectacular icosahedron, the spirit in twenty faces faded,
And he was off to curse, scream, & brood about Mrs. Boyd's thorny cacti:
"Say! I've seen spirits for dogs, uncle shades for mice, ghosts for ghosts.
Where can I find such an insect soul, a Roach's paradise renown, I cry?"
Asked Hector despairingly.
"Where are the spirits for departed roaches, my kin, my ancestral hosts?"
Pleaded the Roach with a sniffle.

62

"From whom am I descended... from whence came my grossest inclinations?
Who should I remember yearly with candles in glass? Who in such glowing toasts?"

XIII

Lorenzo considered Hector's plea, drew upon his expansive poltergeist skills,
And bent a street light onto a garbage heap, scattering 10,000 ghost roaches:
"When in the densest jumble of trash I find placards of waste, simply divine,
Oh, top trash with blasted ketchup on the walls! Everybody sing! Ah Vermin encroaches,"
Sang Hector, joyously.
Call upon that oozing pooh, huddled by a restaurant door, a beloved maggot chorus,"
Crooned the Roach, staring upon the Maggots on pooh.
"La! La! La! La! Putrid sublime. La! La! La! La! We wiggle in grime.
Yah! Yah! Yah! Wretched souls. Yah! Yah! Yah! Our Maggot brains quite porous."

XIV

Celebratory, Hector clutched his heart, blowing out red smear with each "Yah".
And the Oodles company, appalled, bobbed their heads dizzy:
"This hear, with each potato crusted ear: Hector's vomit song to love the unclean.
Here's the city's worst corner; it throws my roach heart into a tizzy,"
Called out Hector, dancing a joyous creepy-crawly.
"Paint the walls ! Paint the walls! Let drip reddened sugar & vinegar concoction,"
Sang the Chorus until the streetlight above exploded all into darkness.

"It's a saddened day if our fate must be grounded in the fake.
Paint the walls ! Paint the walls! We, buried deep by idiocy's
deduction."

XV

With darkness covering the pitchy Chorus, Lorenzo called for Hector to
return,
And the Oodles van, Pietro head out the window, glided towards the
tea house:
"There's not a single light glowing in this house, nor this house, not
this…
Let's glide on fast fuel, lest we hear arias sung by a singing louse,"
Advised Pietro to his van mates.
"With such glorious midnight visitations behind us, there's no need to
stew,"
Said Lorenzo, glowing more than usual.
"This decaying avenue has much to show; let's hold on to all that
essence.
Finding such beloved spirits is what all night dwellers should do."

BOOK 3
Scene 3
Frog Knot Yoga Society

I

Lorenzo was certain that the troupe was closing in on the tea house,
And the Oodles van hung a right onto West of Ville's Main Street:
"Those falls! Those falls! Shall we all stop for lick of cascading water?
Hanging a doggone head out a window is thirsty work; I desire liquid
sweet,"
Bayed Pietro out to a darkened park.
"See the splintered blocks shaped into a train engine, the falls
beyond,"
Continued the parched Mutt.
"The falls beyond pour sweet philters into the creek below in torrents.
Then all shall love you, yes? Better than Dulcamara's elixir... that
potion in a pond?"

II

Pietro growled an opera aria for an audience of one ghost, one mouse,
one roach,
And, much to his delight, Pietro also sang for a quintet of frogs, all in
yogi poses:
"There's few who believe that a ghostly dog might actually sing.
But when hearing his phrases and dotted fermatas, they'll all be
tossing roses,"
Crooned the tuneful, dead puppy.
"Mighty Toads of the Falls, would you like to hear my aria's remaining
strains?"
Asked Pietro, sounding ever so humble.
"No!" said one Frog. "We stretch here in tandem to find our inner
amphibian spirits.

Your hounding strains will disrupt a frog's poise, departing disturbing stains."

III

Lorenzo shot glances at Pietro; the Dog returned a glance at the Ghost,
And Lorenzo calmly approached the stretching, rather vocal Frog:
"We believe, Pietro and I, we found our spirits with more spirit within.
It's the way of ghost-hood… Though, may I say, such an exquisite down dog,"
Said the Opera Ghost to the Frog.
"I must say, without the proper lingo, you bend in such a handsome pose,"
Chimed in an eager Pietro, yet sensing squirrely about the park.
"Such excellent squirms & squats must kick away unwanted scurf.
You've up and down dogs? Please accept guidance from one who knows."

IV

The Knot, one by one, ignored Pietro, delicately breathing in through small noses,
And exhaled trilled chirps like content April peepers, each on a matted leaf, then froze:
"Fellows of the Frog Knot Yogi Society, tonight a gentle vinyasa. Let bones creak.
Salientian sun salutations! Down! Up! Plank! Lower! Breathe! Snaring fly pose!"
Said the exercise leader, as tongues extended long.
"We're on a journey to find the Great Tea House that sits on one plumb street,"
Piped Lorenzo, feeling a little rude for disrupting the solemn mood.
"Desires pluck away at our daily rhythms! I desire to see the old stone abode.

It plagues me so—this craving to return to where my heart once did beat."

V

Sparse snowflakes landed on each planked tongue, adding a little uninvited weight,
And the Knot continued, raising webbed feet for sharp three-legged dogs, sans roam:
"Shanti, our cousins! Shanti, the horned! Shanti, jungle darters! Shanti the toads.
Wherever we may roam, we say peep! Peep! Peep! It's how we peepers say om,"
Said the yogi to the bewildered and much traveled onlookers.
"We are green croakers of the night! Peepers never stressed, though out of season!"
Said the Yogi to Lorenzo, peering over a shoulder.
"November's a cruel set of weeks to call a Knot to rise from slumber, to say peep,
For what's cruel to us must be a rough road for you, Ghost, I dare reason."

VI

Lorenzo noticed the snow piling on the edge of planked tongues,
And yet he continued to share his story with the balanced Yogi Frog:
"My opera house has an angel harp crushed, its Demons released.
I've the glass to restore Chort, Murmur, & Ed back into their own bog,"
Said Lorenzo as clearly as a ghost might express.
"Will-of-the-wisp, you are the opera house host; command this despotic lot,"
Spoke out the Frog with sudden directness.
"I shall call you wisp, for you seem drawn by nonsense instead of will.
Never avoid the ghost-light nor hide in shadows; applaud your spirited spot."

It was to be a tadasana, a mountain pose, for the Knot to emulate,
And, despite the Yogi's soft call, they remained stuck to their matted fronds:
"Dear Master Yogi, now I have the glass, I need bid the tea house farewell.
Then I may return to the Linden to dispatch a perverse trio of operatic frauds,"
Explained Lorenzo to the one seemingly listening.
"Hector, yours is the smallest peak in yogadom, your mountain pose,"
Said Dorabella, demonstrating a spectacular bend in her Tadasana.
"Of all the roaches in my brief life, I see you as one quite spectacular.
Your bend, one must admit, makes you so pretty when on your back fours."

Hector brought his front legs up steady, cupped them, brought both in front of his heart,
And then performed an amazing three-legged roach, while remaining mountainous:
"Dear Dorabella, you are quite the kind Mouse. There's poetry in the grimiest of gutters.
Find it! See it! Roll in it! Think of pages edible! Embrace but be weary of its roughness,"
Said Hector, enunciating the first credo of his weathered manifesto.
"Sweet Mouse, be as gracious for old food as you would for new food,"
Continued the suddenly metaphysical Bug, with a second credo.
"I've a third creed, that I advise all to consider when stomping on sidewalks:
One man's step in poop is another man's relief; quaint apologies for being so rude."

Pietro, in the meantime, spotted what he found to be a handy sycamore,
And he wattled, as in his living days, to the tree, seeking a scent so stray:
"Since you all seem delivered into the famed November froze pose,
I say your statuesque stance says savasana, so I say to all, namaste,"
Said the Yogi, causing the Ghost Dog to freeze in his tracks.
"I shall sit as you command, for I am an honest dog, I am,"
Said Pietro impatient, obedient, obsessed with park perfumes.
"Goodnight!" (Pietro rose...) "Namaste!" (Pietro sat...)
"Sweet dreams (Pietro rose) "Namaste." (Pietro sat...) Ah a Ghost Dog yoga ham."

X

Pietro stretched a quintessential down dog, causing the entire Knot to blush,
And he gracefully made his way to the tree that long had invited his attention: .
"Farewell Spirit! Farewell Vermin Deux! Every dog must have his rooted tree.
Farewell falls! Farewell Yogi Frogs! This one wood shall be my eternal pension,"
Said the Mutt, fading into sycamore trunk.
"Farewell Oodles! Farwell van! This tree seems to be a tighter fit than expected,"
Groaned Pietro and he squeezed his canine girth into the trunk.
"Shall I fade in tail first or shall I tuck my grayed, toothless muzzle?
My earthly time is done... oof... here my tail first... all seems quite misdirected."

XI

Sure as Pietro struggled, morning peeked through November's dense hold on night,
And the hound, facing east, found himself in a uniquely ghost's tribulation:
"Oh Pietro, your rear flashes out from the south side. You might consider a thicker tree.
There, everyone sees your extended ends. Your face shows on the north… all in truncation,"
Observed Lorenzo, twitching his frosted mustache.
"Yes, this was a trial run… a test in haunting geometry, a blessed twist in dog physics,"
Replied Pietro, feeling that he was blushing but, then again, ghost dogs do not blush.
"Perhaps if I should tuck my tail as if filled with guilt, I might just fit within…
Then pull in hind leg just so, then into the tree go I—a lesson in hounding metaphysics."

XII

Snow slipped into freezing rain as the Yogi Frog suggested a Knot savasana,
And the quintet blew bubbles, their weighted tongues pulling them towards the edge:
"There my body draws within; I am left with flapping ears and protruding snout.
Such a coziness within this tree; this warmth I hereby cuddle… pull in… wedge,"
Announced Pietro, with only a fetching face beautifying the sycamore.
"Loosen all your knotted hearts, Peeper brothers in a frozen row,"
Shouted the alarmed teaching Frog.
"Chaturanga, Men! Chaturanga! You're tilting into the river falls' roar.

Stretch through the cascading ice; peace within, no matter wind or snow."

XIII

One after another, the Knot's crooked line fell into the creek below,
And when one plopped into the icy flow, another followed with a resounding plop:
"Knaves in an Esther Williams bubbly outtake, you've no strokes against waves.
Oh gone again! My troop given to biting wind; one by one they plotz... they drop,"
Shouted the Yogi Frog in full amphibian lamentation.
"Pardon my explosion, Master Yogi. Pardon my plea for the right news,"
Nudged Lorenzo once more to the Yogi standing alone.
"Somewhere, amongst this abundance of trees, rests a sculpted tea garden,
Its greyed stones, elegant walls sparking probing brains through block views."

XIV

The abandoned teacher studied the rising river, said his name was Allum,
And, from mumble to scream, let go a season's worth of passion:
"After all these winters, from whence can a bewildered Batrachian pluck a little zen?
Follow the Main uphill, see a flashing yellow beacon calling you with fashion,"
Said Allum, exhausted from the coldness of a failed yoga night.
"Spin your mechanical monstrosity to the right, look for the charmed squirrel,"
Continued the frog, meticulously rolling up his frond.
"Should you reach the Nut Street you can believe you've gone too far.

71

Seek the Squirrel, his postures completely polite, his mannerisms, well, feral."

XV

Allum bent his knees as if preparing for an Olympic-quality dive,
And he offered final directions as he dove headlong into the icy falls:
"The Charmed Squirrel is neither pub nor puck nor psychic,
But facing this conjured fellow suggests kismet & nearby tea house halls,"
Advised Allum, executing a greenish swan dive, degree of difficulty—frosty.
"Be certain the fur-ball phantasm guides you all to the ends of a Plumb Street,"
Added Allum, thumping off blocks of ice.
"He, yes, he alone shall guide you to an exacting corner of your memory.
Reach your sacred halls, with gentle voice winds; bellow softly…
remain discreet."

OLIO
#3
La Ahem Hymn from Ed
Meanwhile Back at the Opera House
A Demon Speaks

So often I've heard it said a demon shall not utter a hymn... not even an Ed hymn. This an idea I'd like to squash as hog's wash, as is Ed's whim. (Wait 'til you see our drift of Pigs.) An Ed hymn asks: Deluge the world with radical kindness. Remember that barren sentiments can lead to a swift kick in the sonnet. Most significantly, given my grave demonic condition, mine hymn is one for tissues, soft, enveloping, soothing tissues. Tonight, I speak for tissues.

I clear my throat. La ahem! Sorry for the flow.

The category for the Ed Hymn is Ed slime. What makes for Ed slime? Antigone's demise... slime! Van Gogh's starry skies... more Ed slime, Butterfly's end... oh the slime. Cat whiskers brushing my pitted cheeks... I am a rotten demon.

Therefore: God bless tissues. Rhinorrhea is my cousin. Gesundheit tissues, Dios de bendiga tissues, Dieu vous bénisse tissues, namaste nose tissues, cheerio booger blow... tissues. I might dare to say shall we keep the evil eye away but I am told that would be me.

The History of Tissues... by Ed. Made for the boys in the trenches... The Great War. Not much great about it but tissues. Tissues flap when you blow, so go the ages. Sponges never flap as so. Empty opera houses lack sufficient tissues, which even the curmudgeon Aristotle would say is tragic, for should there be no sufficient place to blow... this I know. We attended high school together. Aristophanes beat him out for homecoming king and, well... the tissues.

Lear knew where to blow... just at the Dover. Ahab's mate called the right blow, right where the great leviathan blew. No tissues? Well that blows too.

Tissues are the things that bind Ed's hind. I am a bad demon.

Bless your inner Chort! Bless all you Murmur. So ends mine Ed Hymn.

Book IV
Scene 1
Queegueg Café

I

Allum slid towards a river bank, reaching savasana by clunking about the ice,
And he joined an unconscious Knot, with freshly sore knots upon their heads:
"There before icy grace goes a knightly Frog, his grand Knot now gone.
Harpooned they be by very perils we, each ghastly winter, come to dread,"
Mused Lorenzo, churning Allum's directions to memory.
"So now you march to see the Squirrel and the stone-gated tea house door?"
Queried Pietro, left howling from within the tree.
"I say farewell, Mouse, Roach, and fabulous Opera House Ghost.
From within I shall howl 'til this ligneous fellow is sick no more."

II

Pietro's whitened eyes glistened with tears as he made his goodbyes,
And a morning frost layered on his friends glimmered in the November grey:
"Regards to the Charmed Squirrel, for it would be one I would foully chase.
"Lorenzo! Hector! Dorabella! You've brought me to where I wish to namaste,"
Smiled the fading dog, happy with an early morning pun.
"These limbs embrace me, for every dog must have his restful tree,"
Continued Pietro contently.
"I will watch the falls roll over the rocks, pushing away bottles and such.

Move on, friends, no tears Hector; in this park I was born! In this park I
am free."

III

Lorenzo kicked the Oodles van into the most unique case of torque,
And the remaining trio watched Pietro fade into the distance:
"Even I, a Roach, feel my eyes drawing up a shower of tears.
Who has a bug-sized tissue, I plead; I'm in need of snot assistance,"
Said Hector softly, his antennae flapping in the wind like long dog ears.
"Let it all flow, Hector, for parting with travel mates builds knightly
spirit,"
Chimed in Dorabella, she also with teary eyes.
"I see a yellow beacon ahead, a flashing blur fuddled by my mouse
sobs.
What might be the right words for the Squirrel? I don't wish to sound
orate."

IV

The van veered right at the beacon, thumping past red towers,
And its wheels rattled across a road of frosted, dark bricks:
"I expect the Charmed Squirrel shall be more puck than prophet.
Be wary, for there may be some degrading, fossilized tricks,"
Predicted Lorenzo, concerned the bricked road might upend the van.
"One wonders whether words of reason still ring within those
towers,"
Said Lorenzo, reviewing his living days.
"Mornings within the towers' bricked bailey, wrangling over poet Grey,
Those old floor boards creaking under my old Doc Martens at ungodly
hours."

V

Ghostly woolgathering leads to accidents: nay, for the trio, oodles of catastrophe,
And the Van swerved left then right, tossed Hector up on top of a rooftop with click, click, click:
"I need a bugle! I got to get my paws on a bugle, and like Gabriel give it a blow.
Lorenzo's driving madly, sending the Roach flying higher than Old Saint…"
Shouted Dorabella, alarmed by the results of a Spirit's musing.
"We've turned a bricked corner and fly by without any Squirrel sighting,"
Announced the frazzled Mouse.
"Here we spin downhill! Here is the street Allum said was quite plumb.
Here comes Hector, a Roach never lost when the tea house lurks near inviting."

At the Plumb Street's end, where the trees stopped for concrete,
And the Oodles van reached terminus, Lorenzo found the tea garden razed:
"I was a student here; I squatted on harsh days here for lucidity.
All has changed… Now all my senses are teased, scorned & hazed,"
Said Lorenzo, shocked by the latest century.
"No more shoji windows or that old magnificent red door display,"
Said Lorenzo hovering over a busy lot.
"I aspire to move hot air but have none to give… only a slight voice to declare,
That rather than my beloved garden, we've come to the Queegueg Café."

The Oodles van was left desolate on the corner of that Plumb Street,
And the trio entered into vocal mayhem that rocked the café's blank
walls:
"Will that be a small pip, a medium pip or our extravaganza pip?'
"One cup for a Pip of a day... 'I'll have just a pip you pup!'... Father, your
call?"
Said a clerk to a waiting Priest.
"I've a grim sermon to write for a deluge savaging children in the
hollers,"
Replied the Priest, seeking words to confront an unraveling day.
"Make it biblical for such a sermon... make it a leviathan... a whale of a
mocha!
For a sermon tackling the worldly fray... yes... leviathan, which of
which stands larger."

Lorenzo leaned close to the waiting Priest, amazed at so succulent a
carte du jour,
And how so many rose early, drank pastries in a paper cups, talked in
pother:
"Now that it comes to mind, what better morning might deserve a
treat?
Yes, something sweet for you, eh... a frappe with maple for the
Father,"
Called out the enthusiastic clerk.
"Room for cream? Try our special Tashtego Creamer... its drowning in
essence,"
Offered the clerk, while nearby mouse expressed surprise at one guest.
"As a Mouse with poignant eyes, not to mention vivacious brain &
senses,
Here is a familiar man, odd yet quaint and an acquired senescence."

Dorabella frightfully spied a frumpy man busily cleaning his glasses,
And to her amazement, he wore a girdle of green—her own enemy's green:
"Gadzooks! The Green Exterminator fortified with java; may Mouse say forsooth?
Stand tall, green one, face a true and valiant Mouse, you benched stalagmite,"
Said Dorabella to a man whose coffee steamed high like a fog.
"A cheese danish, if you please; gently heated, that's all I ask,"
Said the frumpy man, though Dorabella heard his words quite differently:
"Oh Ho! A Danish you say and you 'Axe'; You say before a small Mouse,
Your tag reading Bernie Hotdessert Nudzh; I see your call for a Danish Axe."

X

Alarmed, the Vermin Gang stormed the Queegueg Coffee and Tea,
And Lorenzo made his friends first wipe ice off their feet on a marline-like mat:
"Hands high, Arabica gluggers, this here is Mouse & Roach, the Vermin Gang.
Put away your fusty teas… gutter your caffeinated sugar water, sodas flat,"
Shouted Hector to an oblivious room.
"Like my great uncle, whose last feat--a grapevine across a counter left to right,"
Continued the Roach to no one paying attention.
"I will nibble at your muffins, mad people! My charms shall tarnish your danish,
For I'm in the mood for a nasty, filthy, revolting, pastry-filled custard fight."

Lorenzo, reacting to Hector's revolting yet ineffective rant, fell into a deep fantasy,
And began a meditation swatting a clerk's buttock with a stale blueberry scone:
"Where's the babka? What of honey cake? Hamantaschen apricot and prune?
A café for coddling picky tongue buds? I say a gobbling venue, you drowsy aitchbone,"
Silently yelled the ghost to all but none.
"I scream internally for precious palettes devouring prepackaged pebbledash,"
Ranted Lorenzo even more deeply.
"Let's hang thin bagel on patrons' noses, set them twirling like Holland's great mills.
Is there, in your menu, a moment of the past for the present to go with frozen eggs and hash?"

XIII

Hector began a grapevine across the counter, hopping registers, tip boxes, Lion's Club mints,
And as he passed, each customer hand slapped down, almost crushing the roach:
"Missed me, fella. Watch me dance to another! Missed me, fella. Watch me solo de pas...
Ah! Say there! No moving before your turn; that would a slapping encroach,"
Said Hector, turning flips and occasionally showing a crafted Charleston.
"Nay shall I suffer like my old opera man, Rodolfo Roach? I think not!"
Taunted Hector, demonstrating hi six-legged chops.
"Poor rhymester Dad, squashed, like many a poet, in a box office dank.

Arabesque for Dad…. five legs up… Oh Dad, crushed by in a chilly heel blot."

XIV

The Roach hopped off the counter's edge, Shouting, "Viva La Tosca!" at mid-flight,
And shouting, "Viva la Great Vermin Rebellion," leapt into a trashcan's confines:
"But these be friendly, confines, like Wrigley, dear frumpy, bespeckled narrator.
I've landed in the soft remains of an abandoned muffin just below plucked grape vines,"
Said the Roach, thrilled with his new lot in life.
"Hector, I've given the Green Exterminator a good nick on the neck,"
Said Dorabella, catching the spirit of the Great Vermin Rebellion.
"Viva la Roach! Viva every little Mouse. Viva the Ghosts a plenty!
I exit into muffin abyss… Oh marvelous muck! Oh beauteous dreck!"

XV

Hector went out with the trash, his new bag pulled shut with a histrionic twist,
And Lorenzo heard the roach's tiny voice call out: "Paradiso! I've found Paradiso!"
"Are you woolgathering again, Lorenzo, being cast about like Bellini's *Sonnambula*?
Dreams end after a fitful sleep; we need repair the angel harp just so,"
Said Dorabella, watching the "exterminator" don a greenish bandage.
"What warmth a ghost's dreams entice if hallucinated robust, imagined bold,"
Responded Lorenzo, ready to leave the café behind.
"The Opera House Demons need to be attended to now, dear Mouse.
Yes, Dorabella! I gather wool because it is Ohio! It is November! It is cold!"

Book IV
Scene 2
Angel Harp Blues

I

The pair quickly exited the café following the best chaos a Ghost could cause,
And inside, befuddled patrons ran in circles with twirling bagels upon noses:
"As the Mouse King as my witness, I was certain he was the Green Exterminator.
He claimed a Danish! I saw his axe! My fists pummeled him in appropriate doses,"
Boasted Dorabella, trying to calm herself as they approached the Oodles van.
"Oh Lorenzo! Pietro's treed! Hector's in the heap! In what shall you leave me?"
Asked Dorabella, meekly but sure why she felt compelled to ask.
"Leave… Leave the Knightly Mouse who put down the Green Exterminator?
In no heavenly heap shall I leave you, nor even in the comfort of an old tree."

II

The pair arrived at the poorly parked Oodles van, its rear tires upon the grass,
And Lorenzo shared what he realized while storming the Queegueg Café:
"It's not a tea that fits my ghostly needs, neither matcha nor mugicha.
Rather, this glass should fit the harp like a T… there's the why for our night stray,"
Said Lorenzo, showing the glass found the hours before.
"Lure Chort, Murmur, & Ed into where the angel harp we did mutilate,"

Continued the Ghost, twirling his semi-mustachio.
"There we'll trap the troubled trio so the harp can once again sing.
But what is this that rests on our wipers; a city letter in script
immaculate."

III

From the West of Ville post, Lorenzo gathered no applause for his
parking proficiency,
And for a special fee, noted the letter, Lorenzo might park better for
$175:
"Such tight quarters for such a voraciously bad brood of musical
brutes.
How to trap such viciousness, such… say who are your city callers?"
Asked Dorabella, seeing Lorenzo distracted.
"So Lorenzo, filling a glass to the T turns to be the quest that sencha?"
Punned the Mouse, with a toothy grin.
"Tell me, Ghost Leader, the Green Exterminator impersonator
scribbled nonsense,
On napkins, something about Golems playing baseball with cats, quite
Dada."

IV

Lorenzo placed the letter back under the wipers, signaled for Dorabella
to enter the van,
And firing up the vehicle with a fantastic ectoplasmic blast, sped up the
wooded Plumb:
"Listen, Dorabella, our letter rattles in the wind like Ravel's snapping
snares.
Wahoo, what a haughty tune, his scrumptious "Bolero"-tapping,
erogenous drums,"
Marveled Lorenzo, now that he found a greater purpose for such a
letter.

"Here's the old sycamore again; bid farewell once more to our solid friend, Pietro,"
Said Lorenzo, growing pleased to be returning home.
"Watch for the motoring buckeyes in the road for they roll in slants and flickers.
The gurgles we hear come from the awakening, grousing, moaning metro."

V

The Oodles van weaved past oblong shops, reaching the inner city's remains,
And found where Hector had discovered the amazing Maggot vocal ensemble:
"Here is that same broke Chorus that astonished us, that we so admired.
What vocals we heard, worm voce all, while calculating a soft womble,"
Said Lorenzo to a confused Maggot coterie.
"Oh Spirit, your memory was of fly generations long since passed,"
Replied one Maggot to Lorenzo.
"You speak of our grandfathers; may they sing in peace… oh Grandfather Mort.
His Grandfather Momentary… his brothers Msec & Micro… Gone! Gone! Gone! Alas."

VI

The successor Maggot pointed his round head to his companions wiggling on a wrapper,
And each companion, seemingly tearing, boldly explained the nature of their committee:
"We're, together, the Maggot Brothers. We repel song, as new generations must rebel.

From our petite porch, we maintain fly and order... We're here inspecting the city,"
Continued the extroverted, bleached worm.
"Join us, Mouse! We've discarded player cards, jacks & jokers stashed in our heap,"
Said the Maggot, twisting in an errant sunbeam.
"Oh too hot... much too hot... the sun reveals the faux world as we deem it.
Join us, Ghost! Sow from weeds... sow with us what flying green bottles reap."

VII

Dorabella quickly ushered Lorenzo back into the idling Oodles van,
And the pair wound their way from the Maggots' peculiar platform:
"Chort, Murmur, & Ed await on stage at your house, the Linden.
Urgency, Spectral Mirage! Vanquish the trio... Your house needs reform,"
Said Dorabella, reminding the Ghost of his quest's purpose.
"My house, indeed! Dorabella, no opera house musters opera without a Mouse,"
Replied Lorenzo, speaking directly to his remaining friend.
"If ever a drama could ensue, it's when a Mouse scuttles center stage.
Then the arias begin, duos, trios alike; they all shriek; they all grouse."

VIII

Reaching the opera house limits Dorabella pitched her demon disposal advice,
And both entered the house finding it all the more dusty, just dusty:
"Dust everywhere yet hardly does one flake rest in the right place.
They've disturbed our dust, Dorabella! They've ruined chains once a lovely rusty,"
Said Lorenzo, examining the wreckage of Chort, Murmur, & Ed.

"Friend Mouse, we've not brought stones from Wall of Wasted Whimsey,"
Said Lorenzo, keeping an eye out for three mischievous Demons.
"We've only this glass shard reminiscent of our night at the arch.
The tea house & pawpaw cover stripped away… our quest seemingly flimsy."

IX

Dorabella considered Lorenzo's frustration for a Mouse-like moment,
And then she sternly looked into her friend's sparkling eyes:
"Lorenzo, official haunter of ye old Linden Opera House, such despair!
I've plans on how to bring Chort, Murmur, & Ed down to size,"
Said the Mouse without blinking a lid.
"First, I say, we call Murmur by snorting trumpets… his attention engrossed,"
Said Dorabella, her plan sounding proud yet esoteric.
"Then, with quick paws, we grab the edge of his repulsive chain of drool.
How does one grab evil by the drool, Lorenzo? By capturing its loudest boast."

X

Lorenzo studied the Mouse's strategy, his growing qualms generating queasiness,
And uncertainty, misgiving, skepticism… certainly clanging doubt:
"Holding a demon's drool seems impractical for certain, but what of Chort?
What plans do you engage for a hooven Demon, clipping through demonic gout?"
Asked Lorenzo ever more the skeptic.
"First shower on the coy; argue Chort hoofs like Kelly or Astaire,"
Replied Dorabella as a matter of fact.

"For every Chort the trickster must be tricked to become our trickster, so say:
'Oh Chort! Such handsome clacking hooves, such tuneful snorts, I do declare'."

XI

Lorenzo could not but laugh at the Mouse's melodramatic performance,
And then queried Dorabella as to how to catch Ed, for he does as he pleases:
"Yes, Ed… Ed may be the trickiest of the party, for barely holds any evil.
By his grotesqueness, we'll lure him with tissue promises for tears & sneezes,"
Advised the Mouse with a wink to the Ghost.
"Mix a cup of bravado with hints of faint praise, enveloped within delicate hankies…"
Continued the Mouse rescue recipe.
"Squeeze the three into the harp's openness then cover with the bluish shard.
We dance the Ta Da dance as we've put away the cranky under a blanky."

XII

Grinning, Dorabella opened her arms wide to show Lorenzo Ta Da paws,
And she nudged, nay cajoled Lorenzo closer to a histrionic finish:
"Need we a gallon of bravado, heaps of praise for Chort or Murmur?
"Need we mounds of wispy snot rags for Ed's presence to diminish?"
Questioned the persistent Mouse.
"Lorenzo, we seem to be running out of space for error or delay,"
Said Dorabella peering into a petite pair of paws.
"Things unpleasant are always creeping about… thorny, knotty…

Stowing the Trio into the harp will be our means to end the fray."

XIII

The pair strategized, finding themselves at the fabled elephant ramp,
And imagined when pachyderms actually passed by these very bricks:
"Far be it in my spirit to question the wisdom of a Mouse,
So here in this passageway, we'll face Demon Chort's tricks,"
Said Lorenzo to the guiding Dorabella.
"So many night I'd settle in this elephant tunnel to let go sniffles,"
Reminisced the Ghost.
"On stages, ghost tears appear as dust; mop a stage, mop away our sobs.
No time for waterworks… tonight all sad emotions… mere piffle."

XIV

Lorenzo began to call to the Demons, inviting Chort's presence first,
And, with a swallow, summoned the most sickening praise he could muster:
"Come comely Chort! Share with us your beauteous bright side!
Flash your hairy hips, your glistening horns, your shimmering lustre,"
Said Dorabella, reveling in her redundancy.
"With what hellions might you sing bass in an opera house, devil Chort?"
Said, Dorabella, laying on fabulous butter.
"You are the magnificent amongst the miserable, eons' mightiest Mefistofele.
Hoot Monterone's curse or the Commendatore's sending Don to a hellish court."

Quite pleased, Chort appeared with blistering fire circling his expansive
horns,
And he wiggled, tossing the flame about as if he were a blazing
Rapunzel:
"You call in appropriate measure, Mouse. Yet where's the spice in this
dust?
Assure me, cheese-gnawer, your praise is not mere motes of useless
brattle,"
Said Chort with more than a tinge of thunder.
"Antlered bud to Beelzebub, I praise honestly through each rodent
pore,"
Assured Dorabella, leading Chort to the damaged angel harp.
"Ease your shouts! Rest from worry! From tunnel to stage, here starts
satisfaction.
The spice you desire lies underneath these angelic keys.. here is its
savory door."

Book IV
Scene 3
Lorenzo by the Ghost Light

I

Chort leaned over the harmonica, nose in the keys, inhaled for a spicier realm,
And Lorenzo aimed at the beast's bottom in order to squish him back into the harp:
"Well, Mouse, here I inhale, relish sulphur but take in solely the fragrance of glass.
Daily, I grift for souls but here, bend like a bad signature, sinking deeper than a carp,"
Complained Chort, horns and head deep within the instrument's opening.
Certainly where a nose might wander, greater curiosities are bound for finding,"
Advised Dorabella, patting the crusted creature on his back.
"Reflection, grand sir Chort, reflection. Can you detect your gruesome reflection?
See yourself eye to eye, an odd Narcissus, admire your ugliness forever binding."

II

With what poltergeist energy he could muster, Lorenzo bumped Chort's behind,
And the insipid fellow, howling, plunged deep into the angel harp opening:
"Wait, heavy Mouse, wait! Delay my exile! Hear my astute dramaturgical plea.
Butts in seats elate in basses phonating bad behavior, plots melodiously flaunting,"
Argued Chort, whose yellow eyes peered from under mouse and glass.

90

"Conundrum, yea, yet hear advice from a renowned demonic aesthete,"
Continued the monster, harmoniously deep.
"Release me from this prison glass; I will bring you singing villains galore!
Then, only then, will this house entertain with an opera night complete."

III

Upon the pane of glass found at the arch, Dorabella mulled over the offer,
And peered skeptically at the Demon struggling within the harp's keys:
"It is your view that ugliness can exist in this house, even characters insipid,
That should make teeth chatter, my pumping blood line freeze?"
Said Dorabella, though understanding Chort's boisterous idea.
"Here I am, villain extraordinaire. Any opera house would want such tense air,"
Replied Chort to the wavering Mouse.
"You plotz upon the glass since you've the weight the floating Ghost there lacks.
Remove the glass… I've spectacle to share… Consider Murmur's grandiose stare."

IV

Lorenzo cautioned his companion, who pressed all her weight upon Chort's head,
And the imp, refusing perdition, called for Murmur to demonstrate his stage qualities:
"These splintered boards demand greater spectacle… volumes of harmonious howling.
Reject him not, for he's a rising matinee idol… his face like a gaudy ocean anemone,"

Said Chort, thinking that he may be close to winning Mice hearts and minds.
"To speak of orchestras, you speak of Murmur, his tuning skills astounding, yay blessed,"
Said Chort, knocking yeoman Dorabella from her sentry.
"He's gifted with enough thick slaver to string one hundred violins. Drool twirling availability for birthdays or football games upon request."

V

Murmur lassoed his demonic colleague around the horns with brown mouth slime,
And, growling, began to pull Chort from the depths of musical muck:
"Cripes, Chort! You're horned anchor havoc! Havoc! I'm crying Havoc! I say let loose the hogs of boar... Urgh, Chort! I believe you're stuck,"
Grunted Murmur, pulling the fiend with all he could muster.
"Gore! Murmur! Gore! The line shall be spoken: 'Let loose the Hogs of Gore',"
Said Chort, breaking a tooth on the angel harp.
"I thank thee, repulsive prompter! Wannabe bard! Let loose the Hogs of Gore!
Brutish this may well be; we keyboard Demons shall launch an opera war."

VI

Swift swine, counting up to three, burst from under the Demon, snorting,
And Dorabella, upon the Demon, was tossed to the right, the glass off left:
"Hogs in the tunnel! Hogs in the tunnel! Great Caesar's Ghost! We've got Hogs!
In a brick-laid burrow made for elephants, galloping Hogs leave us bereft,"

Shouted Lorenzo, dismayed by the turn of events.
"Excellent swine! Tuneful swine! I present The Hogs of Gore, Ghost!"
Said Chort, smirking because his brood smirk.
"I come to you with such commentary not to pose as rascal gasconade.
I say, Ghost, let them croon in the tunnel... you'll be a most gratified
host."

VII

The triptych porkers smiled, ensembled, warmed their giant larynges,
And with a grunt pitch pipe, the Hogs of Gore sang their tale:
"Glorious we, a swelling coro; we'll settle here... your piggy banda,
Our voices echoing phrases Cyrillic, romantic throughout this elephant
trail,"
Sang the harmonious vaudevillians.
"Though Orwellian metaphors, we quadrupeds believe what's said is
said,"
Continued the trio, slipping into a three-part apology.
"Our voices, we fear, verily niggle; true human strains concerns us.
For we're a little green when it comes to singing Verdi; its failure we
dread."

VIII

Stunned by their timidity, Lorenzo complimented the singing trio,
And, delighted to hear music, assured each of their magnificence:
"To fire up things operatic is to risk the rise of tomfoolery.
Yet for such sounds, I believe, it's a worthy risk, sans malfeasance,"
Said Lorenzo to assembled piggily three.
"Sing, Pigs, sing! The mouth of the wolf slathers only to love you,"
Shouted Lorenzo, relishing the return of sound to his house.
"String, Murmur, string. Gather enough glop for virtuosic pit band,
Vibrato, Chort, vibrato! Better to trill and thrill than to swelter and
stew."

IX

Dorabella was certain that Lorenzo's mind twisted in horrifying manner,
And she kept a keen eye on the two Devils, though only seeing the tops of their toes:
"We've a piece essential to your house; his tenor shrieks for an opera night complete,
Perfection... our Alfredo, our Rodolfo... please hear how his explosive patter goes,"
Said Chort, whipping off Murmur's excess.
"Do you mean to add Ed as the troubled lover then hear echoes of Milan nights?"
Asked Lorenzo of nodding Demons.
"As I once rose for the aromata perfumes of marinara, I concur by condition.
By condition, I properly request you plug this lamp, let glow my Ghost Light."

X

The lamp lit up, casting much needed shadows over the palatial stage,
And Dorabella sparred with the darkness ahead, her silhouette large like an elephant:
"All demons beware... Mephistopheles, we know you're up to no Gounod.
 Oh... dear... by my whiskers... I now recall I have forgotten the quest most relevant,"
Said the Mouse to rows and rows of torn red cloth seats.
"Poor Fred still wanders the riversides, grasses, perhaps alleys for his Soprano Love,"
Said the Mouse spying Demon Ed.
"Yes... mustachio Lorenzo... I fear a mouse wanders. I fear these demons' evil perspire...

To make evil, frightening brave sopranos, tenors, bassos, mezzos &
mice in droves."

XI

The Mouse, from close study of Demon Ed, feared Lorenzo would be
ghosted,
And that by virtue of their cunning, three Demons would rule this old
house:
"These are the masters of gunk, basting you exotic with pleas thick as
ghee.
Be wary! They sing from experience… be they play rogue, rascal, or
louse,"
Warned Dorabella, eyeing a sniveling Ed particularly.
"I fear this here fellow's the Green Exterminator under an Ed nom de
plume,"
Whispered the Mouse to her dearest friend.
"These spawns need return to innards of Franklin's shattered wind
howler.
Then, along with sooty marinara, sweep their gunk out with ragged
broom."

XII

Chort stepped from the angel harp, smearing on dirt to add to his foul
toilet,
And shining his horns with Murmur spit, he continued his arty sale:
"I'm engaged to gunk, that much is true, but you, Mouse are hardly
gunk.
Every operatic night needs a scoundrel; there's where I blithely
regale,"
Said an encouraged Chort.
"Murmur may warble but he hardly ever chortles; that's where I shall
rune,"
Continued Chort, without snivel or snort.

"Ours will be nightly acts in four, arias episodic, tessitura thrills, vibrato wild.
We humbly promise: we shall not regale the house with bestial tunes."

XIII

Dorabella watched Lorenzo welcome such an ensemble into the Linden,
And she spewed out, without reservation, as the night's madness spread:
"So singing maggots! So dog-swallowing trees! So speeding Oodles vans home.
So opera ensemble pigs! So bad basso Demons? But Lorenzo, where's my Fred?"
Argued the Mouse distraught at a harsh night result.
"Where's my beloved Brother Fred? Off with magical monsters, I suppose,"
Said Dorabella to the wizened Ghost, replying:
"He's secure within earthen matters, ready for a hoofing downbeat,
In an opera house of his own, sweet Mouse, where his earnest love grows."

XIV

They sat center stage, awaiting a curtain rise, though it lay frayed on house seats,
And Ed, hiding in a far off wing, crooned: "Butterfly! Butterfly!" in snotty notes:
"Will there be magic this night, Ghost? Will faeries muster up tricks on fops?
Or will they fling out Bellini's pirates or a hunt for Shostakovich's nose?"
Asked the Mouse, settling in to hear a Demon's opera.
"They will bring what is to be brought! The operas of Chort, Murmur, & Ed,"

Said Lorenzo, ready to watch the unwatchable, to hear something.
"Let's tune the angel harp, let Linden's leaks set the tone for tonight's
show.
I think they've got it, Mouse! I think they've got the right operatic
cred."

XV

Chort plugged in the Ghost Light, its beams blanketing Lorenzo for the
night,
And the Pigs trio vocalized borrowed scales from Murmur's furrowed
brow:
"So, where are the faeries? Bring on the faeries! Hurrah, Robin
Goodfellow.
I hear the hum of hasty chorus, tones horned off-pitch. No faeries...
HA... then ciao!"
Called out a hopeful Mouse.
"Stay, Mouse friend. It's far away from hot solstice, I fear, but this light
do trust,"
Said Lorenzo, with a poltergeist-grip on Dorabella's tail.
"There's faeries in the city. Wonderful, beautiful faeries. They set the
city aglow.
Yet hear the Demons' songs! Hear the chorus! Here's my latest, more in
dust."

About the Author

Les Epstein is a poet, playwright, opera librettist and educator. His work has appeared in journals in the United States, Philippines, India, Canada, Ireland and the UK, including Slant, Muse McMaster, The Bacopa Review, The Clinch Mountain Review and Empyrean as well as the anthologies Heat the Grease (Gnashing Teeth Publishing) and Pain & Renewal (Vita Brevis Press). He is the author of Sleep Cinematic: a Golem's Quartet (Gnashing Teeth) and Kip Divided (Finishing Line Press). As a playwright, his work has been staged by such theaters as The Belfast Maskers (Maine), Greenbriar Valley Theater (West Virginia), Stone's Throw Dinner Theater (Missouri) and the Roy Arias Studio

(New York City). He contributed libretti for two operas, Barefoot (1997 premiere) and Miss Lucy (2011 premiere). Cyberwit released a collection of his short plays and libretti (Seven) in 2018. Epstein's bi-lingual collaboration with Claudia de Franko, Llorona of the River is available through Silver Birchington plays. He received undergraduate degrees in English and Theater from Otterbein College, an MA in English from Miami University (Ohio) and continued with studies in literature at New York University and in Theater Education at The Ohio State University. He completed his teacher training at Mary Baldwin College. In addition to work with theater,, opera and ballet companies from North Carolina to New York City, he spent ten seasons as Education Director and Production Coordinator for Opera/Columbus and another seven as Executive Director for the Children's Theater of Winston-Salem, before settling in as a teacher with Community High School (Roanoke) for which he has staged more than forty productions.

www.ingramcontent.com/pod-product-compliance
Lightning Source LLC
Chambersburg PA
CBHW060333130626
46553CB00003B/1001